# The
# Product
# Manager's
# Handbook

**Linda Gorchels**

*Printed on recyclable paper*

NTC Business Books
a division of *NTC Publishing Group* • Lincolnwood, Illinois USA

Library of Congress Cataloging-in-Publication Data

Gorchels, Linda.
    The product manager's handbook / Linda Gorchels.
        p.   cm.
    Includes bibliographical references and index.
    ISBN 0–8442–3669–1 (hard)
        1. Product management. 2. New products—Marketing. I. Title.
HF5415. 15.G636     1995
658.8—dc20                                                95–11300
                                                              CIP

Published by NTC Business Books, a division of NTC Publishing Group
4255 West Touhy Avenue
Lincolnwood (Chicago), Illinois 60646–1975, U.S.A.
© 1996 by NTC Publishing Group. All rights reserved.
No part of this book may be reproduced, stored in a retrieval system,
or transmitted in any form or by any means,
electronic, mechanical, photocopying, recording or otherwise,
without the prior permission of NTC Publishing Group.
Manufactured in the United States of America.

5 6 7 8 9 BC 9 8 7 6 5 4 3 2 1

# CONTENTS

# PREFACE

## Competing with tomorrow

You've heard it said that "the more things change, the more they stay the same." So it is with product management. Companies are facing turbulent times. Change is rampant and organizational structures—including product management structures—are being ripped apart. But through all the turbulence, there remains a need for entrepreneurial spirit, for an ability to work with and through other people, for a clear and focused direction, and for a willingness to be a hands-on professional. That's the true essence of product management and the tying theme for this book.

Product management has long been viewed as one of the more effective organizational forms for multiproduct firms. The advantages of this form are numerous and frequently documented. First, it provides a dedicated champion for a product, brand, or service.

Second, a healthy internal competitive environment can be created. Third, by championing a number of offerings, a firm can more quickly respond to shifting customer loyalties. And, finally an opportunity is provided to readily assess candidates for promotion to higher management levels.

Nevertheless, the effectiveness of product management is contingent upon several factors. If we expect product managers to truly champion brands, they must be engaged in both day-to-day decision issues and in developing the strategic future paths of their offerings. Although some companies have created a hierarchical product management structure to do this, effective product management in the future will result from a horizontal decision-making structure. Product managers will play a major role in most product-related decisions, while relying on specialists to carry out many of those decisions. The emphasis will be on matching customer needs with corporate capabilities through the development of specific products and services.

## Organization of the Book

The four sections of the book address these essential aspects of product management. The first section is devoted to the need for entrepreneurial spirit and the ability to work with and through other people. Section Two covers the planning required for a clear and focused direction. The last two sections highlight the need and tools required for a product manager to be a hands-on professional.

## Leading without Direct Authority

The book's first section, on the role and operation of product management, discusses the importance of entrepreneurial thinking and the ability to influence others in the absence of direct authority. In particular, several examples of "heavyweight" product managers are cited to demonstrate both the visionary entrepreneurial role of product management as well as the interpersonal leadership role. Product managers are charged with the success of a product or product line. Still, they typically have no direct authority over the individuals producing and selling the product. Much of the work of a product manager is through various departments and cross-functional teams, almost as if the product manager were operating a business within a business. The overall responsibility of the product manager is to integrate the various segments of a business into a strategically focused whole while maximizing the value of a product by his or her knowledge of changing market needs and championing the processes involved in bringing the product to the served market.

The way product managers are "positioned" in a company can have a significant impact on the true role they play, regardless of the responsibilities put in writing. A critical issue for management to decide is what balance between administrative and entrepreneurial functions it wants to assign to product managers. Product managers with a relatively low perceived status cannot become true change agents. On the other hand, product managers with a relatively high perceived status must have the skills and respect required to perform effectively.

A primary objective of product managers is to get all functions to focus on the market, the final customers. Therefore, they must interact directly with various functions in the organization, including sales, operations, finance, customer service, and top management. Chapter Three describes some of the typical relationships, and provides suggestions for improving the relationships.

## Annual Planning

Section Two provides an overview of the annual marketing planning process. By continually asking yourself where you are now, where you want to go, and what marketing techniques can be used to get you there, you focus on the most important factors surrounding the planning process. The two chapters in this section provide tools and suggestions for developing the annual marketing plan for a product or service. The planning process moves from the vision and corporate strategy (where the emphasis is on developing and leveraging core competencies) to the specific product/market tactics to attain customer satisfaction (with the emphasis on customer-specific needs).

Leveraging the company's core competencies becomes critical in new product development, and product managers need to understand how they can benefit from this leveraging. For example, 3M was able to leverage its technology used to develop film for signs into film built into laptop computer screens. Hewlett-Packard benefited from using similar mechanisms in ink-jet printers and in fax machines.

Chapter Four contains worksheets for analyzing your markets, your competition, and your product's performance history. Several questions are listed to trigger ideas and perspectives frequently forgotten or overlooked during the planning process. The outcome of the analysis is an identification of the problems and opportunities that need to be addressed within the marketing plan. Chapter Five describes how to write marketing objectives and positioning statements, and ends with an example plan outline, profit and loss statement, and media calendar for the marketing plan.

## Hands-On Professionalism

Sections Three and Four emphasize the hands-on activities of typical product managers. Section Three highlights the analytical skills a product manager needs for product line evaluation. For example, the trade-offs between line extensions and completely new products need to be considered and weighed. Nabisco was successful in line extending to Fat Free Fruit Bars and 7-Up was successful in its Cherry 7-Up extension. However, other line extensions, such as New Coke, were not successful.

The section moves from evaluating an existing mix of products to using that evaluation for strategically planning new products, to the actual development and launch of the new products. The discussion of the development process (Chapter Eight) addresses the product manager's role in idea generation, screening, concept development and testing, prototype development and evaluation, prelaunch, launch, and project evaluation.

The three chapters in Section Four cover the functional skills a product manager needs for marketing decisions. Chapter Nine provides the basic considerations for setting prices and making price changes. Since an important part of a product manager's marketing function is pricing a product to balance profitability and customer satisfaction, it's important to understand the components of pricing decisions. Also, by looking at pricing decisions in the context of overall marketing planning, it may be possible to avoid price competition through creative tactical decisions. For example, Zebra Technologies developed a low-priced, no-frills printer in lieu of reducing the price on its main product. Hewlett-Packard modified the price sensitivity toward its Deskjet printer by repositioning it against dot-matrix rather than laser printers. Chapter Ten provides a summary look at the product manager's role in marketing communications, distribution, product support, and marketing research decisions.

## The Future Is Now

The final chapter examines three current trends in product management: (1) the emergence of product management teams; (2) more specialized focuses in product management positions; and (3) the transition to business unit manager. Each of these will be tested in the future as companies strive to improve the competitiveness of their organizations. The rules of competitiveness will also change with the growth of global megabrands and the dramatic metamorphoses of distribution channels and logistics management.

Corporations will continue to experiment with reengineering, downsizing, flattening the hierarchy, and creating teams to handle processes such as new product development—i.e., experiment with the concept of the horizontal corporation. Proponents of the horizontal organization claim that the structure reduces supervision, combines fragmented tasks, eliminates work that fails to add value, and focuses company resources on its customers. Strong product management fits easily into this mold, as long as it's not allowed to become a hierarchy within a hierarchy.

So, the more things change, the more they stay the same. And product management will continue to provide a viable and critical function for the competitiveness of many firms in the future.

## Acknowledgments

My interest in product management began several years ago when I realized that the term meant significantly different things to different companies. Several people contributed to this growing awareness, including participants at my product management workshops at the University of Wisconsin-Madison Management Institute. I found numerous examples of non-traditional approaches to the subject, and widely varying success factors. This book highlights some of those findings.

There are many people I am grateful to for the development of this book. First, I want to recognize the team at NTC Publishing. Their suggestions, insights, and constructive recommendations have been invaluable. Second, I would like to thank my husband for supporting my effort by allowing me the time necessary to write this book. Finally, I want to record my gratitude to my mother for instilling in me a desire to achieve and continually strive for new challenges.

# SECTION ONE

## THE ROLE AND OPERATION OF PRODUCT MANAGEMENT

As companies grow, with more products being sold to increasingly diverse sets of customers and competing against diverse new sets of competitors, the need frequently arises for a product management organizational structure. In this type of structure, product managers are given the responsibility of managing a set of products or services that face different competitors and different customer constraints than may be true for other products and services in the company.

Determining if product management is the right structure depends on a number of considerations, including the technical knowledge required to market a given product, whether a company's products require distinctly different approaches to "going to market," and the culture of the organization. Once a system is installed, clarifying the roles of company personnel with whom product managers routinely interact is important.

The product manager is a generalist who must rely on numerous functional specialists to develop and market the product line. The product manager is the liaison among the functional departments within the company as well as between the company and the sales force and the customers for all product-related issues. As a result, some understanding of mutual expectations is appropriate.

On an ongoing basis, product managers exchange information with the sales force. They represent the voice of the customer at internal meetings on the product line in question. And they need to plan for current and future product activities that benefit the company as a whole.

This section discusses the evolution of product management, provides suggestions for selecting the "right" product managers and managing the system effectively, and demonstrates the need for product managers to be cross-functional leaders.

# 1

# THE NEW PRODUCT MANAGEMENT

The overall responsibility of a product manager is to integrate the various segments of a business into a strategically focused whole, maximizing the value of a product by coordinating the "production" of an offering with an understanding of market needs. To accomplish this, a product manager needs a broad knowledge of virtually all aspects of a company along with very focused knowledge of a specific product or product line and its customers. In fact, product managers manage not only products, but projects and processes as well.

Procter & Gamble has been credited with the creation of the product management concept. In 1931, Camay soap was languishing while Ivory soap was thriving. A P&G executive suggested that an individual manager be assigned responsibility for Camay, in effect, to pit the brands against each other. This brand-management system was so successful that it was copied by most consumer packaged goods companies.[1]

Product management is a matrix organizational structure in which a product manager is charged with the success of a product or product line, yet has no direct authority over the individuals producing and selling the product. Much of the work of a product manager is through various departments and cross-functional teams, almost as if the product manager were operating a business within a business. (See "The Life of a Consumer-Brand Product Manager.")

There are both advantages and disadvantages to product management. On the plus side, a product manager provides dedicated attention to a product line. This results in better information on the customers, competition, and strategic potential for that group of products. In addition, since the product manager must necessarily interact with the various operational units of a company, the position can provide a good training ground for young executives.

On the other hand, one common criticism of the product management structure is that it is a "fast-track" or "stepping-stone" position, overemphasizing short-term results. It also promotes the perception that product management skills are more transferable than product and industry knowledge. In addition, product management can cause conflict because the product manager has limited functional authority over many parts of the development, marketing, and sales of the product, but may nevertheless have bottom-line responsibility. Finally, product managers might focus on the product almost to the exclusion of the customer.

Despite these limitations, product management (or some variation) has found its way into virtually every type of industry, going well beyond the traditional consumer-product brand-manager position. Even within fast-moving consumer packaged goods companies product management has evolved. Because of the increasing level of internal brand cannibalization and competition for

# The Life of a Consumer-Brand Product Manager

Tracy Carlson, senior product manager for Lever Brothers' Wisk detergent, spends an inordinate amount of time with stains. In an effort to move her brand to become the best-selling liquid laundry detergent in the country, she has to convince consumers of the superiority of her product over Procter & Gamble's Tide. Like her counterparts at other consumer-product companies, Carlson is responsible for nearly every aspect of her product.

More than being simply champions for their brands, product managers are viewed in some ways as running their own little businesses. They not only oversee product development, but also monitor advertising and promotion, as well as negotiate to obtain shelf space from retailers. With current product proliferation, manufacturers concede that there are few lasting competitive advantages from which to attain market dominance. Therefore, sensitivity, intelligence, and intuition are important traits for product managers facing these battles.

But the real challenge of the job for product managers like Carlson is often simply getting the product onto shelves. A glut of new products has made retailers reluctant to open shelf space without generous inducements from manufacturers like Unilever. The inducements include paying for in-store displays, fees for mentioning the product in-store advertising circulars, and paying for the increased processing costs of warehousing the new products.

Carlson will not reveal the Wisk marketing budget. But she said that in general the proportion of consumer-products budgets that go for trade and consumer promotions has risen from less than half to as much as three-fourths, with the balance going to advertising.

Source: Condensed from "High Stakes for Product Managers," *The New York Times,* December 4, 1989, D1-D7.

---

resources, along with media fragmentation and a higher level of retail and consumer sophistication, product management is being stretched into different "shapes."

## Product Management Today

Product management as an organizational form has moved into a variety of business-to-business firms as well as service organizations such as financial institutions and hospitals. Most large banks have product managers for credit cards, deposit services, trust operations, and commercial cash management services.[2] Property/casualty insurers have begun to utilize product managers for highly competitive, rapidly changing lines such as workers' compensation and auto insurance.[3]

Hospitals have also experienced success with the structure. A recent study published in the *Journal of Healthcare Marketing* reported that hospitals with product line management outperformed those without it on virtually all performance indicators, including occupancy rate, gross patient revenue per bed, average profit margin, and return on assets.[4] Not surprisingly, the implementation of product line management increased with level of competition and hospital bed size. Other health care studies found that product line management in hospitals offered the benefits of increased accountability, elimination of duplication of services, and a better market orientation. The limitations included a possible increase in costs (because functional management was not eliminated) and an increased need for more timely and accurate data.[5]

Even though traditional product management has had its successes, companies have increasingly modified the concept of product management to incorporate a focus on the customer. This has taken many forms. Some service firms have created what is in fact segment management (even though the product manager title might still be used). Hospitals, for example, might have a product manager for women's services. Financial institutions might have a small-business product manager or an "affluent market" manager. Deregulation in financial services has contributed to this latter phenomenon. Interest-bearing checking accounts, money market funds, affinity credit cards, and an explosion of other product offerings attempt to appeal to increasingly smaller market segments. This, along with the availability of more sophisticated technology, has changed the focus of product management at banks as discussed below:

> [In 1991 alone], banks launched about 700 new affinity programs, and customers opened 7.5 million new affinity accounts. The aim of product proliferation has been to satisfy an increasingly divergent set of customer needs. To keep track of these divergent needs, banks have invested in customer information file technologies that permit segmentation across many dimensions, only one of which is product. The data generated by CIFs have accelerated the growth of market-segment-focused strategies.[6]

Segment management has been successful at several banks. (See "Segment Management in Financial Services.") Simply shifting the emphasis from products to segments, however, will not eliminate some of the problems that can exist in a matrix organization. Both—or neither—can result in an enhanced understanding of customers and an ability to satisfy their needs. It requires a commitment to make it work.

First, there must be a clear understanding of the basic rationale for product management as an organization form. Product management is generally most successful for companies with several products having similar manufacturing but different marketing requirements, particularly when the same product cuts across several divisions or customer groups. Second, top management must be committed to the product management organization and provide the structure and tools to make it work. And, finally, the right people must be selected and developed for the job.

## Product Management Tomorrow

Product management will continue to evolve to meet the needs of business circumstances and of the particular company employing it. Consumer goods product managers, for example, will find it necessary to be more involved with the trade as retailers gain more knowledge of and "influence" with consumers. Consequently, they will need to think more in terms of category management. Category management involves looking at a line (i.e., category) of products as they might be evaluated by a market segment (i.e., retailer). To accomplish this, product managers might need to work together as a category team. Or a category manager position might be established to oversee all products and product managers related to a given market segment.

## Segment Management in Financial Services

Banks that have traditionally used product managers have generally assigned them to groups of deposit products, home equity loans, mortgages, insurance, etc. Unfortunately, these products are not always complementary, and they might even be considered direct substitutes by consumers. Therefore, banks such as Sovran Financial and Bank One/Texas have experimented with segment management.

Sovran Financial Corp., a holding company for four Middle Atlantic banks, reorganized its marketing structure to replace product management with a market segment emphasis. Sovran had attempted a relationship marketing strategy before the structure change, but found it difficult to implement with an organization by product. Therefore, in 1988, it reorganized by individual market segments, such as the "affluent market." The segment management design allowed Sovran to capture what it referred to as "share of wallet," which increased from 38 percent to 46 percent in Virginia and from 44 percent to 62 percent in Tennessee.

At Bank One/Texas, one of the product managers is the small business market segment manager, responsible for developing marketing programs to support the branches and sales force in bringing in new small businesses to the bank. This position has enabled Bank One to package products appropriate for a specific segment's needs.

Source: Condensed from "Eric Berggren and Robert Dewar, "Is Product Management Obsolete?" *Journal of Retail Banking* 13 (Winter 1991/1992): 30; Lauryn Franzoni, "Product Managers: Finding the Right Fit," *Bank Marketing* 23 (May 1991): 28+.

Another trend that might affect the future role of product managers is the use of product management teams. As companies continue to escalate their involvement with total quality management (TQM) and other quality principles, product management teams (PMTs) will appear in some companies. Global companies will have cross-border product business teams responsible for leveraging capabilities throughout the world. These will be "virtual teams," which do not meet regularly on a face-to-face basis and are not located in the same country. Although project teams have been very successful in new product development, the appropriateness of *ongoing* teams in charge of existing products will have to be carefully thought out and structured before implementation.

Regardless of the organizational changes product management may undergo in the future, successful product managers must thoroughly understand the needs of various segments within the market, appreciate the corporate competencies available in the company, and be able to leverage these competencies to meet market needs. In other words, the ultimate goal of the product manager will be customer satisfaction obtained by being a cross-functional leader in the firm.

## The Product Manager's Job

The product manager's job is to oversee all aspects of a product/service line to create and deliver superior customer satisfaction while simultaneously providing long-term value for the company. To accomplish this, there will be various day-to-day, short-term, and long-term activities. Day-to-day activities provide the foundation for the job of the product manager and usually absorb 40-55 percent of a product manager's time; 20-30 percent of the time will be devoted to short-term activities; and 15-25 percent will be allotted to long-term tasks. (This of course will vary depending on the time of the fiscal year, the relative proportion of new versus mature products managed, as well as a host of other variables.) These are goals. Unfortunately, the reality is that many product managers spend too much time "putting out fires," to the exclusion of strategic planning. (See Figure 1.1.)

A recent national survey of product managers showed that a significant proportion of product managers spent much time responding to sales force requests and expediting products through other departments but wished they could spend less time on those activities than they currently do. On the other hand, this same survey found that product managers spent little time developing long-range strategy for products and contacting customers to understand future needs/applications but wished they could spend more time in these ways than they do now.[7]

### Day-to-Day Duties

On a day-to-day basis, the product manager might have the following responsibilities:

- Maintain a product fact book
- Motivate the sales force and distributors

### Figure 1.1 The Product Manager's Balance of Activities

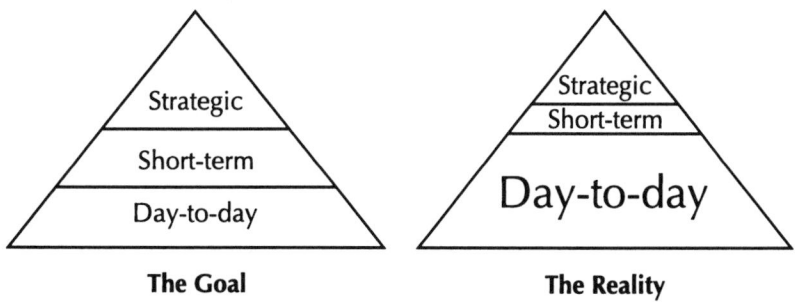

The Goal    The Reality

- Collect marketing intelligence
  - Competitive benchmarks
  - Trends and opportunities
  - Customer expectations
- Act as a liaison between sales, manufacturing, research and development (R&D), etc.
- Control the budget and achieve sales goals

### Short-Term Duties

On a short-term (e.g., fiscal year) basis, the product manager might have the following responsibilities:

- Participate in annual marketing plan and forecast development
- Work with advertising departments/agencies to implement promotional strategies
- Coordinate trade shows/conventions
- Initiate regulatory acceptance
- Participate on new-product development teams
- Predict and manage competitors' actions
- Modify product and/or reduce costs to increase value
- Recommend line extensions
- Participate in product elimination decisions

### Long-Term Duties

On a long-term (strategic) basis the product manager might have the following responsibilities:

- Create a long-term competitive strategy for the product
- Identify new product opportunities

• Recommend product changes, enhancements, and
introductions

Historically, the product manager's job varied somewhat between
consumer and business-to-business firms. Consumer product managers typically managed fewer products and spent more time on
advertising and sales promotion. The target markets were generally
larger (millions rather than thousands or hundreds), with a greater
potential for diversity. Business product managers tended to be more
involved in the technical aspects of the product or service and spent
more time with engineering and the sales force.

However, the gap between the two types of product managers is
lessening. Fragmentation of consumer markets has escalated, resulting in greater product proliferation and parity products, for which
consumers perceive little distinction in features or quality and usually make purchase decisions based on price. Trade satisfaction is
becoming more critical as mass merchandisers and other "category
killers" (such as Wal-Mart, Home Depot, and Office Max) are gaining momentum. As a result, consumer product managers are finding
themselves more involved with salespeople and the trade (e.g., retailers). On the business-to-business side, product managers are finding
a growing need to introduce advertising to their firms and to create a
more solid positioning against an ever-increasing number of competitors. Market (as opposed to product) knowledge has become a
key determinant of successful differentiation.

# References

1. Zachary Schiller, "The Marketing Revolution at Procter & Gamble,"
   *Business Week,* July 25, 1988, 72.

2. Jean E. LeGrand, "A Product in Need of Management, *Bankers Magazine* 175 (November/December 1992): 73+.

3. William J. Wichman, "Product Management as a Marketing Strategy," *National Underwriter,* July 29, 1991, 10+.

4. G. M. Naidu, A. Kleimenhagen, and G.D. Pillari, "Is Product-Line Management Appropriate for Your Health Care Facility?" *Journal of Health Care Marketing* 13 (Fall 1993): 8.

5. Ibid., 10.

6. Eric Berggren and Robert Dewar, "Is Product Management Obsolete?" *Journal of Retail Banking* 13 (Winter 1991/1992): 27+.

7. Based on information from a proprietary survey conducted by the author.

---

## Checklist: The New Product Management

---

✓ To assure that product managers focus on the long-term value of a product, do not view the function as a "fast-track" or "stepping-stone" position.

✓ Be careful not to lose sight of the customer as you strive to create competitively superior products and services.

✓ If you have specific groups of customers who require unique products, or if you must combine standard products in unique ways to meet the needs of these customer groups, consider segment management as an alternative to product management.

✓ Expect the role of product manager to continue to evolve to meet current business challenges. Category management and the use of product management teams will be tested by companies striving to improve competitive performance.

✓ Balance your activities among day-to-day, short-term, and long-term activities, to avoid the trap of constantly "putting out fires."

# 2

# INTRODUCING PRODUCT MANAGEMENT AND MANAGING PRODUCT MANAGERS

The product manager's job can be one of the most challenging in a company. The position is endowed with great responsibility but, in many cases, limited authority. Product managers must rely on the support and performance of many others in the organization to achieve product performance goals, yet they have no control over those functions. Clarification of objectives is imperative for the successful introduction of a product management structure in an organization. Unfortunately, many companies introduce the title "product manager" because their competitors have such a position, but they lack understanding of what the position entails.

There are four elements involved in initiating product management. First, the company must assess whether product management is the appropriate organizational form and, if it is appropriate, decide what reporting structure it will have. Second, the company must clearly specify the responsibilities of product managers as well as other integral functions in the system. Third, characteristics of successful product managers must be identified, with suitable personnel recruited for the product management openings. And, finally, there must be a system for developing and evaluating product managers. Each of these will be discussed in detail in this chapter.

## Assessing the Need for and Structure of Product Management

Product management can be an appropriate organizational structure when a company's product line has grown to the point where a functional structure no longer works. There might be more products than a single marketing manager can handle, even though these could flow into a common market through the same channels. Or the company's products might be so different from each other in terms of competition and customer groups that they must be handled differently. Or technical or sophisticated product knowledge might be required to meet the needs of the market. In this case, the product manager might be involved in the development and marketing of a product line across various divisions or markets. (See Figure 2.1.)

On the other hand, there are subtle variations that might be appropriate under different circumstances. (See Figure 2.2.) If the industry's products are primarily "parity" in the minds of the customers, a traditional product manager structure might result in pressure to create artificial differences simply for the sake of differentia-

## Figure 2.1 Traditional Product Management Organization at a Consumer Products Firm

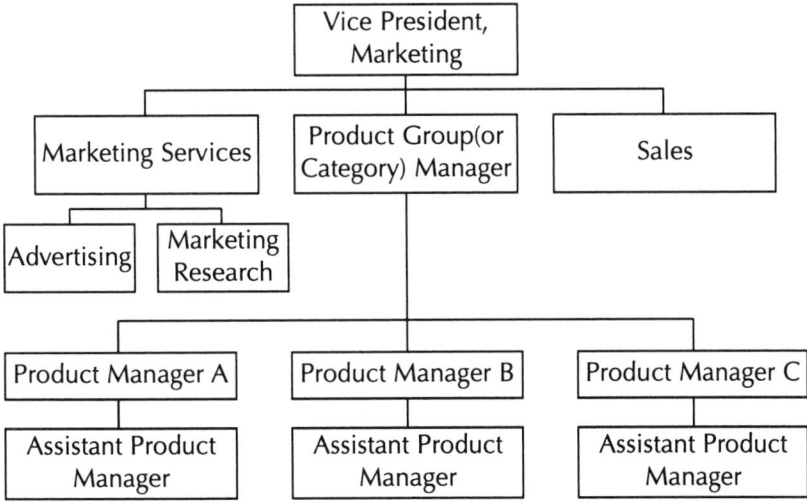

tion. In this case, a market or segment management approach might be preferred. Market managers are used when a company needs to develop different markets for a single product line. Focus is on developing the market rather than on taking the product to market. The market manager would "bundle" and/or adapt combinations of a company's products to fit the needs of select market segments. There might or might not also be a need to have "special products" managers in conjunction with segment managers.

A variation of market management is key account or national account management. With the emergence of "category killers" and other large customers, key account managers have been given the responsibility of working with major accounts to determine how products can best be adapted to meet their needs. If product man-

## Figure 2.2  Appropriate Organizational Structures for Various Product/Market Types

| Product/Market Characteristics | Possible Organizational Structure |
|---|---|
| Many products going to a limited number of market segments. The products require focused attention to be fully successful. | Product management |
| Company sells to a variety of market segments with preferences for various product sets. The products might not require elaborate customization, but the "bundling" of products is unique to the market segments. | Market or segment management |
| The same situation as above, but there is also a need to develop some new products for various market segments. | Segment management with "special products" managers |
| The company sells to a few large customers with differing needs from the rest of the customer base. | Key account management |
| New-product efforts are time-consuming and critical for the company, to the point where a special position is created exclusively to handle new products. | Product development manager or new products manager, possibly (although not necessarily) part of a technical department |

agers are spending an inordinate amount of time handling special requests for major customers, a key account position could focus on the "special requests" and work with the product manager on product adaptation.

## The Impact of New-Product Development

The last major consideration in organizational structure is related to new-product development. Although most product managers spend a significant part of their time on new-product development activities, some companies choose to have a separate new-product manager position to handle the specifications and design of products, with the product managers following through with the marketing activities. Although this is less common (and perhaps less desirable if customer input is an afterthought), it is an organizational form that can fit certain needs.

## Implementing the Global Structure

For global companies, there's an additional level of complexity. Companies must decide whether a single product manager has global authority for a product, whether product managers should interact with country managers, or whether there should be country-specific product managers. At minimum, the product manager will be involved in cross-cultural teams charged with leveraging the skills of different parts of a global company located in different parts of the world. As Whirlpool CEO David Whitwam said in an interview with *Harvard Business Review:*

> The only way to gain lasting competitive advantage is to leverage your capabilities around the world so that the company as a whole is greater than the sum of its parts. Being an

international company—selling globally, having global brands or operations in different countries—isn't enough.

Let me use washing machines as an example. Washing technology is washing technology. But our German products are feature-rich and thus considered to be higher-end. The products that come out of our Italian plants run at lower RPMs and are less costly. Still, the reality is that the insides of the machines don't vary a great deal. Both the German and the Italian washing machines can be standardized and sim-plified by reducing the number of parts, which is true of any product family. Yet when we bought Philips, the washing machines made in the Italian and German facilities didn't have one screw in common. Today products are being designed to ensure that a wide variety of models can be built on the same basic platform. Our new dryer line has precisely this kind of common platform, and other product categories are currently being designed in the same way.[1]

## Reducing Hierarchy

Most product managers are part of a marketing or marketing/sales department, usually reporting to a marketing or product manage-ment director, a marketing or product management manager, or a vice president of marketing. Product managers frequently have no one reporting to them. In larger firms, however, product managers might have assistants and associates reporting to them, as well as authority over some functional subordinates. Some product man-agers have eight or more people reporting to them directly. If there are to be staff under the product manager, it's usually best to provide information processors, coordinators, or analysts, rather than proliferating pyramids of assistants and associates—in effect, creating a hierarchy within a hierarchy.

Hierarchies are designed to prevent mistakes, but they also take away individual responsibility, creativity, and risk taking. That's why so many management gurus have espoused variations of the horizontal corporation, with an emphasis on providing better products and services for the end customer. Product managers and product management teams are consistent with this philosophy if they are linked to customer satisfaction (as they should be) and given the authority to make relevant decisions regarding their product lines. (See "Taking Product Management in for a Tune-Up.")

## Specifying Responsibilities of Product Managers and Others in the Firm

To minimize the potential for miscommunication and misunderstanding and to increase the chances of a successful product management structure, management must thoroughly explain to key managers exactly how the organization concept will work and what the underlying rationale is for moving to it. It's important to specify not only the roles of product managers, but also the roles of the individuals with whom they commonly interact. Let's take a hypothetical example of a company with three product managers, a marketing services manager, a marketing research manager, and regional sales managers. (All of these people might report to a marketing director or a vice president of marketing/sales.)

Typically, the product managers would recommend and establish strategic guidelines for their products, obtain market intelligence on their customer segments and products, provide input to sales for the closing of selected accounts, and play a major role in product/service

## Taking Product Management in for a Tune-Up

There are several variations to the traditional product management structure. For example, Procter & Gamble has added "category managers" to oversee product managers handling competing products. By settling disputes and approving expenditures, resources are utilized more effectively. In addition, the category management process is more consistent with the category management thought process of retailers.

Colgate-Palmolive might have been the first company to use category management. Others, including General Foods, Campbell, and Nabisco, have tried category management to shift from a product focus to a market focus.

Kraft has moved much of the authority over promotional expenditures from the product managers to more central control. The desire is to leverage the Kraft name rather than individual brands and to reduce the amount of dealing.

At Black & Decker, parallel systems of product management and channel management bring together the production and distribution of products more effectively. Now the product manager has ultimate authority over the marketing programs in the channels.

R. J. Reynolds has developed brand teams to coordinate the various specialists involved with specific products. The teams have the responsibility to move the company closer to the customer.

Source: Adapted from Kevin Higgins, "Firms Tune Up Their Management" and "Category Management," *Marketing News* September 25, 1989, 2+.

development, modifications, and elimination. The marketing services manager would provide support to the product managers in terms of communication materials and handle company-wide promotional and public relations activities. The marketing research manager would contract out or conduct marketing research activities required to fully understand customer needs and competitive capabilities and provide input into company growth and acquisition opportunities. The regional sales managers would provide the day-to-day motivation and management of the sales force and support the product managers in the introduction of new products.

Many product managers (particularly in business-to-business companies or in the service sector) are hired for their technical expertise with a specific product or service. Therefore, the roles of the product management function and the related operational functions will need to be clarified. For example, the product manager might supply customer and competitor data in support of a recommended new product but leave the actual design to the design staff.

Although the above description of responsibilities would not be appropriate for every organization, it's important to think through the related responsibilities and overlaps. By providing a summary of role responsibilities before introducing product management, uncertainties about the organizational structure will be minimized.

The way product managers are positioned in a company can also significantly influence their role, regardless of the responsibilities put in writing. A critical issue for management is to establish a balance between product managers' administrative and entrepreneurial functions. Product managers with a relatively low perceived status cannot become true change agents. On the other hand, product managers with a relatively high perceived status should have the skills and earned respect required to perform effectively.

A major service-sector firm, introducing product management for the first time, created a task force charged with establishing a model of product manager responsibilities along with the responsibilities of ten support areas (plus senior and business unit management) as they related to product management. The product managers were charged with many of the specific activities listed previously. An abbreviated summary of the responsibilities of the ten support areas is listed in Figure 2.3. Once the structure of product management is installed, management must select the right people and monitor and coach their activities to make sure they stay on track.

## Figure 2.3 Responsibilities Established by a Major Financial Services Company

**Senior vice president**
- Setting overall direction and priorities of the organization
- Overall resource allocation

**Business unit manager**
- Approving annual product business plans and budgets
- Determining product resource allocation

**Product development**
- Conducting feasibility studies of new products/major enhancements
- Coordinating the development and introduction of new products

**Market research**
- Measuring, tracking, and reporting product market shares
- Conducting product research as requested

**Marketing and communications**
- Developing and coordinating product-related marketing and sales communication
- Assisting in the development of marketing plans
- Executing marketing plans

**Sales**
- Prospecting for new business opportunities
- Closing sales

**Operations**
- Routine customer support and service
- Providing product operational efficiency

**Corporate relations**
- Identifying new business opportunities, and retention strategies
- Coordinating corporate business development plans

**Personnel**
- Developing and implementing a product manager professional development plan
- Conducting product manager specialized skill training

**Quality assurance**
- Assisting in the development and monitoring of quality standards
- Providing process improvement evaluations

## Characteristics of Successful Product Managers

There is no ideal profile of a successful product manager. However, several traits, skills, and experiences are frequently identified as related to product management success. Frequently cited traits looked for in product managers include an entrepreneurial attitude, leadership, and self-confidence. Acquired abilities should include organizational, time management, and communication skills. Sales proficiency and technical competence are also important in many industries. Prior experience depends on the needs of the product management position. If highly technical, engineering-oriented knowledge is required, a background in engineering is appropriate. If an understanding of customer applications is desired, a sales background in the industry is appropriate. If knowledge of large-market trends and competitive positioning is a necessity, marketing research and/or advertising experience are desirable.

The appropriate characteristics depend partly on the culture of the organization and the role expectations placed on the position. Some product managers provide (and are expected to provide) a coordinative role; others may be more directive; and still others take on a leadership role. Specifics for each follow below.

Product managers who are coordinators primarily function as administrators to assure deadlines are met and requests are carried out. Coordinative product managers are more likely to deal with budgets than plans. Product managers who are directive not only coordinate projects but also develop product plans. Product managers who are leaders are more entrepreneurial and become more active in the strategic planning of products and services for the company.

Part of the difference depends on whether the product managers work for consumer or industrial product manufacturers. A study of senior marketing executives from Australian companies with a product management organization found differences in management expectations between consumer and industrial firms. Marketing executives from consumer goods firms tended to view product managers as coordinators or implementers of strategy to a greater degree than was true for industrial firms. On the other hand, a greater importance was placed on forecasting and competitor intelligence for industrial product managers than was true for consumer product managers. This is partly because of the wealth of syndicated data available about consumers that is absent in many industrial channels.[2]

This same study highlighted some problems with the product management concept (PMC).

> Those companies who expressed dissatisfaction with the PMC were asked in an open-ended question to explain their reasons. The range of reasons embraced the following: too much time spent on day-to-day matters with not enough planning and searching for new opportunities; PMs not sufficiently entrepreneurial; not enough authority over sales department and poor communication with sales force (the most frequently mentioned responses); poor understanding of PM role; inexperienced PMs; authority-responsibility mismatch.[3]

## Developing and Evaluating Product Managers

Product managers need a variety of knowledge, including product/industry knowledge, business knowledge, and interpersonal/management knowledge. Beginning product managers typically spend most of their time in gathering and organizing information on the product, its customers, and the competition; product knowledge is paramount. As they gain experience, the focus shifts to more comprehensive business knowledge including finance, marketing, and strategic planning. At the same time, they develop team building, negotiation, communication, and leadership abilities.

Many companies believe it takes from three to five years to build an effective product manager. According to Bill Meserve, a principal at the management consulting firm of Temple, Barker & Sloane Inc., training and motivation are critical at this time, and career development must be an obligation. "The formal approach used at one 3M division is based on a written career development document and scheduled annual reviews, which are separate from performance appraisal. Primary responsibility for monitoring career development rests with senior marketing management or a separate marketing council."[4]

For product managers to be effective, they need to build bridges throughout the company and be cross-functional leaders. Therefore, in the selection and development of product managers, this ability to transcend functional lines must be considered. The downfall of several product or brand management systems was the establishment of a product manager as caretaker of the product, with an emphasis on "safe" results. Product managers were charged with immediate results rather than the creation of long-term customer value. When this happens, product managers focus on improving their own position rather than that of the company's product. According to William Weilbacher in his book, *Brand Marketing:*

> In the end, the brand manager is forced by the brand-management system to pay more attention to career management than to brand management. Brand championship and brand advocacy are replaced by actions that make the brand man-

ager look good to management, no matter what the long-term effect upon the brand or the perceptions of the consumers who buy it.[5]

Appropriate evaluation criteria depend on the performance expectations of management. Sales and/or profit goals are fairly common measures of performance. However, if profit is a measure, it's important to distinguish between profit contribution and bottom-line profit. Profit contribution is the amount of product revenue remaining after subtracting all of a product manager's direct, controllable, or relevant expenses. This contribution to overhead (CTO) figure is a fairer assessment of performance than is fully allocated profit, because CTO minimizes the concern over the validity of the allocation methodology. Obsessive attention to allocating overhead against each product often consumes effort that could be better spent elsewhere. This isn't meant to imply that total overhead doesn't need to be covered. The CTO goal is established to cover anticipated overhead allocations but doesn't hold product managers responsible for overhead increases beyond their control.

Some companies implementing TQM (total quality management) have opted to minimize individual performance measures and focus on company performance. This does not have to be an either/or decision. Performance measures can be made to accommodate both by weighting the relevant evaluation criteria consistent with company philosophy.

In addition to financial measures, product managers may be evaluated on some combination of other factors, such as the following:

- Successful introduction of new products
- Market share defense or growth
- Customer satisfaction indexes
- Attainment of company-specific goals

## References:

1. Regina Fazio Maruca, "The Right Way to Go Global," *Harvard Business Review* (March/April 1994): 137.

2. P. L. Dawes and P.G. Patterson, "The Performance of Industrial and Consumer Product Managers," *Industrial Marketing Management,* 17 (February 1988): 73–84.

3. Ibid., 83.

4. Bill Meserve, "The Changing Role of Product Management," *Electronic Business,* January 9, 1989, 146.

5. William Weilbacher, *Brand Marketing* (Lincolnwood, Ill.: NTC Business Books, 1993), 123.

## Checklist:  Keys to Product Management Success

✓ Recognize product management as an organizational business form, not as an isolated job function.

✓ Prevent product management from being done in the absence of market management. Otherwise, you run the risk of being production-driven rather than market-driven.

✓ Develop an information system of cost, business, and market information according to the relevant products or product lines.

✓ Clarify the roles of product managers and the roles of those with whom they routinely interact.

✓ Push product managers to evolve from being solely product specialists to being cross-functional leaders.

✓ Establish performance goals that reflect company expectations and provide the tools (budgets, people resources, approval authority) to achieve the goals.

✓ Select product managers with the skill set appropriate for the culture, expectations, and role responsibilities for your company, and provide additional training as required.

# 3

# THE ROLE OF PRODUCT MANAGERS IN THE ORGANIZATION

A product manager, almost by definition, is a generalist who must rely on numerous functional specialists to get the product or service to the customer. These specialists can be internal or external to the company. The presence of internal support groups (such as advertising and marketing research) means that the product managers can be less technically skilled in these areas and place greater emphasis on managing. However, the product manager's control over the internal groups may be less than for an external group because there is no authority. A charge-back system can provide more budget control for the product manager as well as relate costs more effectively to products.

A primary role of product managers is to get all functions to focus on the market, the final customers. Therefore, they must interact directly with various functions in the organization, including sales, operations, finance, customer service, and top management. The extent of interaction will vary by company and the experience level of the product manager. (See "Product Managers in the Electronics Marketplace.") This chapter discusses some of the typical relationships. A recent survey asked product managers to indicate the extent of contact they have with a variety of areas on a scale from 1 (no contact at all) to 5 (very high level of contact). (See Figure 3.1.) The groups with which product managers had the greatest level of contact were sales, research and development (R&D), and customers. The mean or average responses for each area are shown in the right column of Figure 3.1. The percentage of respondents who indicated that it doesn't apply because there are no people in the respective area is shown in the left column.

## Figure 3.1 Product Manager Contact with Selected Groups

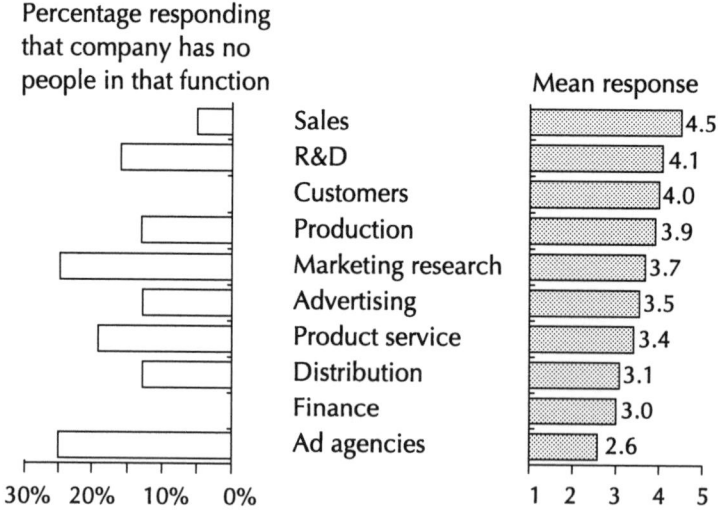

## Product Managers in the Electronics Marketplace

The electronics field is known for short product life cycles and fragmented customer segments. Competition and price pressure are intense. Facing these challenges, the product manager must be able to work with and through a variety of individuals.

The product manager's position will, of course, vary by company as Bill Meserve points out in his *Electronic Business* article, "The Changing Role of Product Management":

> At one components division of General Instrument Corp., product managers function mostly as coordinators between engineering product development and marketing, and between marketing and sales. They have direct responsibility for product line advertising and promotion budgets, but only provide marketing input to product development projects, which are initiated and managed by engineering. Hewlett-Packard Co. product managers, in contrast, are frequently the focal point for new product development. They prepare the product development plan, authorize its implementation and monitor its progress.

Regardless of the role given a product manager by a company, the product manager must develop management skills to be able to lead teams in product development and product marketing. This involves a number of things. First, the product manager shouldn't be afraid to admit ignorance. Even though most technical product managers do have significant backgrounds in their fields, chances are they don't have the technical skills of the existing engineers on the team. Second, it's important to know when to intervene. Although it's essential that the team learn to work together, especially in the new product endeavors, the product manager still has ultimate responsibility for the success of the product line.

These skills are built over time. According to Bill Meserve:

> Beginning product managers with focused responsibilities need specific knowledge about the company's product and competitive offerings. As job experience and responsibility increase, the focus of skills building shifts to functional areas like financial analysis, promotion, pricing design, new product development and strategic selling. And when professional responsibilities progress to even higher levels, management skills become central. Product managers learn to build a team, achieve consensus, negotiate agreements, measure performance and handle personal relationships. Companies such as Allen-Bradley Co., 3M Co. and E.I. du Pont de Nemours & Co. supplement education with direct customer interaction, mentor relationships and cross-functional training to enhance product management skills.

> Source: Adapted from Bill Meserve, "The Changing Role of Product Management," *Electronic Business,* 9 (January 1989), 143-146.

Depending on the company and situation, the product manager will play various roles in terms of support activities. With regard to field sales, the product manager will answer questions from the field, assist on sales calls as needed, provide product information to simplify the sales process, suggest various incentives for new products, and/or develop literature and other customer pieces to help further the sales effort. With regard to distribution, the product manager might work with distributors or agents, suggest alternative channels, and/or expedite shipments. Figure 3.2 shows some of the groups with which product managers frequently interact. Those in bold type generally have the highest interaction. The presence of internal support groups (such as advertising and marketing research) means that the product managers can be less technically skilled in those areas. Each area is discussed in this chapter.

## Figure 3.2 Product Management: Primary Role Influencers

## Sales

The product manager plays a major role in helping salespeople accomplish the objectives of the company (not to mention the objectives of the salespeople themselves). The nature of the relationship varies according to the culture of the organization and the positioning of product management. A coordinative product manager is likely to be heavily committed to sales support and "putting out fires." The position won't generate a desire on the part of sales to provide market intelligence or push the product. At the other extreme, an authoritarian product manager who expects to provide minimal support to the sales force will get minimal support back from them as well. This type of product manager might attempt to use home-office authority to "force" sales cooperation and can severely damage the trust and respect required for a cooperative effort.

### Gathering Market Data from the Sales Force

Salespeople provide a critical link to the customer, and effective product managers appreciate their need for this knowledge. Consequently, salespeople must be given an easy and efficient way to share market knowledge with product managers, and be motivated to do so. With the growth of sales forces equipped with laptop computers, bulletin boards and electronic mail (E-mail) can be significant tools in gaining market feedback. Fax lines, toll-free numbers, and traditional print mechanisms can also be used. Regardless of the method used to collect the information, a standard intelligence report form simplifies the process for both the salespeople and the product managers. Once market data is received, the product manager must recognize the salespeople for their contributions as well as demonstrate to the sales force that the information is being used to their advantage.

The development of sales forecasts is generally the domain of the product managers, but forecasting frequently cannot be completed without the input of the sales force. Salespeople might be requested to estimate sales in their territories in total or by customer and/or product. If the information is broken down by account, it is likely to include an estimate of the probability of attainment. The forecast will be given to the regional or national sales manager, collated, and forwarded to the marketing department. The product manager would work in concert with the marketing analyst to arrive at a realistic forecast for the product line.

### Communicating with Salespeople

On an operational level, product managers will spend a moderate amount of time on the phone with salespeople and prospects. Sometimes the calls are requests for price adjustments or special deals that require product management approval or authorization. Other calls will be questions about product attributes. The more itemized the product fact book (see Chapter 6), the more efficient a product manager will be in providing the answers. Even if salespeople have received the information previously, it is often quicker and more efficient for them if the product manager provides the information on the spot.

That does not mean that the product manager should not also provide the sales force with written information. Salespeople should be informed of any product or marketing change that affects their relationships or negotiations with customers—before the information reaches their customers! Mailgram, fax, special delivery, and similar techniques are useful for high-priority information.

Many companies require product managers to spend a certain amount of time (e.g., 25-30 percent) making customer contacts, possibly on calls with salespeople. These sales calls provide an opportunity to learn more about the customer, or on some occasions to help close a sale. However, there must be clarity prior to the call about the specific role the product manager is expected to play.

Most of the operational activities will not appear on the marketing plan, although they might be part of annual performance objectives (e.g., percentage of time spent in the field). What should be included in the marketing plan are budgets for travel expenses, any special incentive programs (for spurring sales of products that aren't achieving objectives or for introducing new products), or any activities undertaken as part of territory redesign or sales force changes.

## Sales Training

Sales force training can cover a variety of issues: sales skills, company data, product knowledge, and market and competitive intelligence. Although teaching sales skills per se will not typically be part of a product manager's responsibilities, the product training they do has to fit within the framework of the selling process, and the market and competitive intelligence has to be presented in support of this process.

As an example, assume that five elements are included in a company's standard sales training process: (1) planning, (2) establishing trust, (3) qualifying needs, (4) providing customized and visible solutions, and (5) building partnerships. The product training and the role of the product manager should fit into this process.

### *Planning*

First, what information will help the salespeople in the function of planning? They need to know who is most likely to buy the product.

Instead of describing the primary and secondary target markets, the product manager should profile the "ideal" account, suggesting specific customers, if appropriate. If non-customers need to be cultivated, salespeople need to know the types of uses, applications, and functions appropriate for the product. For example, a company selling flat panel display screens might direct salespeople to engineers in specific industries that require a monitor with graphics clarity.

### Establishing Trust

Second, how will the product manager help establish trust with the customer? If a new product is being introduced, the product manager has to demonstrate that the internal support systems are already in place, that the product has been tried and proven, and that customer orders can indeed be filled if sales are made. Promotional support aimed at "getting a foot in the door" of non-customers can also be shared with salespeople, along with tips on effective use of support material.

### Qualifying Needs

Third, what information about the customers must the salespeople obtain to qualify needs? What does the salesperson need to know about the prospect to determine the appropriateness of the sale? Customer satisfaction results from the best match between product benefits and customer needs. If the salespeople "successfully" sell to the wrong people or for the wrong applications, the revenue will be short-lived. Therefore, the product manager must provide customer-friendly questions that enable salespeople to assess the fit before closing the sale.

There should be questions about how prospects perform the function(s) provided by the product, what tolerances are required, what applications they would have for it now and in the future, etc. The questions should not simply push the prospect toward a sale, but rather indicate whether the prospect has a true need for the product (thereby screening out inappropriate prospects). For example, a college textbook product manager responsible for a line of products to be sold to university professors will need to provide questions that assess teaching philosophy, level of rigor, and content preferences of the faculty. The product manager selling flat panel display screens may need to determine whether the screen is used in bright sunlight or office light, whether the primary usage is text or graphics, and whether simple or complex software is involved.

### Customizing Solutions

Fourth, how can salespeople use the answers from the preceding questions to develop customized and visible solutions for the account? This requires a product manager to look for creative ways to demonstrate a product's competitive edge. (See Section 3.)

### Building Partnerships

Fifth, what assurance is there that this product will increase the partnership already established between the customer and the salesperson? In other words, why should the salesperson believe the product will perform as claimed? What motivation is there for them to sell it? For an existing product, the best proof is past sales success. For new products, a bit more persuasion is necessary. Results from test marketing or beta testing, statements from sales managers or other salespeople indicating their success in a roll-out region, sales that you, as product manager, have personally made, or trade shows and lead generation programs in place can convince salespeople that the product is worth their time and effort to pursue. In addition, financial and nonfinancial motivators should be considered. Higher commissions, better bonuses, and desirable contests can work under the right circumstances. Nonfinancial motivators could include customer input suggesting that less sales effort is necessary to be successful, the ability to sell the product along with another product with a minimal increase in selling time, or unquestionable proof of competitive superiority.

A portion of the training might also include a motivational explanation of the need for and use of market intelligence by product managers—and how providing this information can help the salespeople. A standard intelligence report form can be built into a call report, designed into the menu system on a computer, or included as part of the expense form. Because this information typically comes into sales management or sales administration, a process would need to be established to send a copy of relevant product-related data to the appropriate product manager. The type of information deemed useful for submission could include the following:

- New-product announcements by competitors
- Effective and ineffective approaches to selling a product
- Changes in competitive strategies
- Unusual product applications by customers, especially if they indicate a trend
- Perspectives on market trends that might affect company strategy

## Operations and R&D

Product managers of both service products and manufactured products are dependent on operations to create the right product at the right price and delivered at the right time for customers. Whether operations refers to underwriting, loan management, manufacturing, or logistics, a close working relationship is critical.

## New-Product Development

Perhaps the most visible interaction a product manager will have with operations is during new-product development. R&D will need to assess technical feasibility; manufacturing will need to evaluate future efficiency and productivity; procurement might need to be involved with make-versus-buy decisions; and overall capacity considerations will need to be taken into account. The role of the product manager will be to represent the voice of the customer, balancing corporate return on investment (ROI), customer satisfaction, and manufactured cost. Mutually acceptable standards for quality and customer service will need to be established so that manufacturing and marketing strategies are complementary rather than conflicting.

## Strategic Interactions

The product manager can also be involved in strategy sessions with the operations function, separate from new-product development. During these sessions, the product manager will present marketplace problems and/or competitive moves that might trigger ideas for new products and highlight discussion on future capacity needs. This is also the time when product managers learn of technology looking for a market and are encouraged to think of ways to incorporate new technology into existing or planned products in a way that is acceptable to the market. For example, when Ford first developed front-disc brakes, there was concern about how to introduce them into cars given that there would be an inevitable price impact. They decided to introduce them as an upscale option on expensive cars until the price could be driven low enough through mass production to be appropriate for any vehicle.

> The most important lesson was in marketing. Disc brakes were, in principle, not much more expensive to produce than drum brakes; they weren't made of gold. But we were going down the manufacturing learning curve, and were thus comparing costs with a very old design. We had to find a way to get the new brakes paid for without looking dumb.
>
> We solved the problem by choosing an expensive car where the customer would not care quite as much about price, making disc brakes an upscale option for the Lincoln. . . . Once production was automated, the price began to drop. Today, the cost difference between a disc brake and drum brake is minuscule.[1]

The product manager must work continuously with operations to improve and enhance the product line. This requires that a product manager have at least a basic understanding (if in a manufacturing environment) of material scrapped due to worker error, the time it takes to set up a production line, and other operations performance measures. In insurance, product managers need to understand basic underwriting guidelines. In financial services, product managers need knowledge of the secondary market for loans and various financial ratios.

Product managers are frequently involved with operations on cost-reduction projects. Because product managers are expected to bring market insights, they have to focus on ways of reducing costs that will not compromise the perceived value of a product. Cost reduction should not be fleeting. That is, care must be taken that the cost savings are not temporary, with the inevitable result of other costs going up in the future.

Other operations-related activities a product manager might undertake include the following:

- Leading synergy sessions to ensure that all functions are moving in the same direction
- Encouraging discussion of technological advancements that could affect future new products
- Establishing task forces to conduct value analysis on existing products
- Monitoring productivity improvements
- Fostering teamwork to enhance productivity on an ongoing basis

## Customer and Product Support Services

Customer service as a function can exist in marketing, warehousing, sales, or some other department, depending on the organizational structure of the firm. The product manager should both gather information from customer service representatives (CSRs) on product performance and supply information to them to increase customer satisfaction with the product line. Part of the added value for many products is the service level provided by the company. The product manager has to ensure that the service standards are established, understood, and attainable by the service staff.

For service standards to be attainable, CSRs require training. Product managers might request support from the company's human resources function, include CSRs in the product training done for the sales force, and/or develop specific training for them. The more important service is as part of the product's competitive differentiation, the more important it is for product managers to take an active role in making sure the training happens.

The handling of warranties, for example, will require clarity among CSRs. If the warranty specifies 30 days, and a complaint is received on the 31st day, what leeway do the CSRs have in deciding how to handle it? What leeway should they have?

## Finance

Product managers must work with finance to achieve a balance between the way products are costed and the market price desired. Customers don't care what internal cost allocation mechanism a company uses to set a floor for pricing. Their concern is simply whether a product has sufficient value given the competitive alternatives available. Although all costs must be covered to remain profitable in the long term, contribution pricing in concert with market segmentation or product life cycle decisions can be valuable. For example, pharmaceutical companies use contribution pricing to determine how long to sell an old product once a new one has been introduced.

> Often new drugs are introduced that are more effective or have fewer side effects than older drugs, but the older drug still may be marketed. . . . Then the price would fall. The company would discontinue the product when it no longer makes a contribution. It may discontinue sooner if it can use existing capacity to produce products with a higher contribution.[2]

Product managers must also rely on finance to provide line-item information for the budget, pro forma income statement, and/or product balance sheet. By negotiating what information is critical for decision making, both functions can operate more effectively. The relevance of specific costs varies by situation and depends on the decision to be made. Product managers who can work with finance to ferret out the appropriate costs will be in a better position to make the right decisions.

## Marketing Communications

Whether dealing with an internal advertising department or an external ad agency, a product manager needs a general understanding of promotional alternatives to be able to evaluate copy and media recommendations effectively. Typically, product managers will determine what positioning they want for their products, and the communication of that positioning will be left to the functional specialists. Product managers need to describe the target market they are trying to reach as precisely as possible so that the advertising groups can use that information to select the appropriate media and media vehicles.

If there are several product managers working for a company, they must consider the relative merits of advertising the company as a whole and positioning the various products independently of the company. A number of companies are moving to an umbrella approach to branding, in which the company name, reputation, and position is being emphasized as much as or more than the individual brand. Product managers and the advertising specialists can discuss the relative merits of each option and come to an agreement prior to investing heavily in advertising.

If a product manager can choose between an in-house and an external agency, which one should be selected? Obviously there are several factors to consider. An external agency can be preferable for the product manager who needs an outside viewpoint, faces resource constraints internally making it difficult to meet deadlines, and/or wants to take advantage of an agency's potential for mass media buying. On the other hand, an internal department might be the right decision if the product manager needs to capitalize on the expertise of a very specialized market, has the necessary skill in-house, and wants more control over the total process.[3]

There are several factors involved in agency selection. (1) What types of promotion, in addition to advertising, might need to be done? Many companies, particularly in business-to-business situations, need direct-mail lead-generation programs, trade show coverage, or special sales promotion techniques. (2) Does the agency understand the target and have the appropriate talent to speak the language? This does not mean that a technical message needs to be written by a technical person. In fact, this could be completely wrong, because the focus should be on benefits rather than features. However, the copywriter needs to understand how to translate features into appropriate benefits for the customer. (3) Should a large or small agency be hired? Typically, the most effective arrangement is for the client size to match the agency size, and it is better to be the big fish in a small pond than the reverse. (4) Will the agency be expected to help with marketing, research, and/or strategic planning? If so, this might narrow the pool of potential agencies.

## Marketing Research

Although product managers must necessarily have good information on the market and the competition, they are not usually experts in data collection and analysis. That's why much customer research is farmed out to either internal research departments or external research agencies. Product managers can also take advantage of the marketing research supplied by many advertising agencies or even some media publications.

## Customers

Customer contact is an expectation for virtually all product managers. Consumer-goods brand managers usually reach customers through focus groups and other research techniques. Business-to-business product managers are more likely to contact customers while on calls with salespeople, although marketing research is growing in importance for that group as well. The critical point in meeting with customers is to be open to both shortfalls in existing products and long-term future needs. As difficult as it is, product managers must visualize innovations that anticipate and satisfy unmet needs.

## References

1. Don Frey, "Learning the Ropes: My Life As a Product Champion," *Harvard Business Review* 69 (September/October 1991): 54.

2. Robert W. Koehler, "Triple-Threat Strategy," *Management Accounting* 72 (October 1991): 32.

3. Ralph S. Blois, "Do You Really Need an Agency?" *Sales & Marketing Management* 140 (October 1988): 120.

## Checklist: Fitting Product Managers into the Organization

✓ To be most effective as a product manager, focus on being a generalist who can accomplish work through other people and functional departments.

✓ Position yourself with the sales force so that you're viewed as neither strictly sales support nor corporate dictator.

✓ Understand how your activities fit into the sales process.

✓ Be prepared to represent the voice of the customer in meetings with operations and R&D, and demonstrate at least a minimum understanding of operational techniques and standards.

✓ Don't be afraid to question and critique the work of your internal or external advertising agency.

✓ Allocate a significant portion of the time you spend with customers gathering information on future product needs and applications.

# Case One

## Heavyweight Product Managers

During the 1980s product managers began to appear at more and more automotive companies. The motivation for this change was the growth in international competition (today more than twenty auto companies are global), the increasing complexity of the products, and more demanding, sophisticated customers. Product managers (called "large product leaders" at Honda and "program managers" at Ford) were challenged to create not only functionally superior cars, but also cars that are distinctive and embody a certain personality or "feel" consistent with future customer needs.

This last aspect, bringing in the customer, is where the product manager is most critical. The auto companies had previously used matrix structures, coordinator committees, cross-functional teams and other structural mechanisms to improve product development, but these were frequently inward-focused, with possible inclusion of *current* rather than *future* customer desires. External integration is an important and difficult task of the development process. Unless a company makes a deliberate effort to integrate customers into the development process, it is likely to create products that are technologically advanced and offer good value, but fall short with sophisticated customers.

### Ford's "Program Manager" Structure

Ford is one company that had success with this organizational concept. The Taurus, introduced in 1985, was designed to be a family vehicle with sophisticated European styling, handling, and ride. Its success was due to Team Taurus, the cross-functional group responsible for this product. The effectiveness of the team became the catalyst for organizational change at Ford. Shortly thereafter, it formalized the "program manager" concept that evolved out of the Taurus experience.

The structure reinforced cross-functional integration at both the strategy and operational levels. In particular, marketing people (led by the program manager) began to meet directly with designers and engineers. Previously, their involvement had been through reports and memos. The program managers themselves were given greater responsibility for product planning and layout.

As this organizational structure continued to grow, the strength of the program manager position increased, as did the effectiveness of the product development process. Several products that were developed out of this structure followed the market success of the Taurus: the Lincoln Continental; the Thunderbird Super Coupe; the Probe; and the Explorer.

As time went on, Ford management discovered that integrated development required more than a cross-functional team. It became clear that simply assigning a project leader to a team did not guarantee product integrity. The effectiveness of the program manager was the missing link.

When markets were relatively stable, companies could achieve product integrity through strong functional organizations. The ability to achieve superior product integrity now depends on the leadership of the product manager. The product manager becomes the thread tying all the pieces together, filling in the gaps and ensuring that the final product is consistent with the original product-customer concept—with a special effort placed on understanding what customer wants will be at the time a new product is introduced rather than what they are right now. This person must be able to understand:

- what the product does (performance & technical functions);
- what the product is (configuration, component technologies);
- who the product services (target market); and
- what the product means to customers (character, personality, image).

### Characteristics of Heavyweight Product Managers

Of course not all product managers provide the same level of effectiveness. Kim Clark and Takahiro Fujimoto, in their *Harvard Business Review* article, "The Power of Product Integrity," differentiate between "heavyweight" product managers and "their lighter-weight counterparts." According to their research in the automotive industry, many product managers are functional workers rather than cross-functional leaders. They lack influence outside of product engineering, have little or no contact with working-level engineers or with marketing, and act primarily as facilitators and coordinators. As a result, they spend much of their time going to meetings, reading reports, and writing memos.

Heavyweight product managers, on the other hand, function as the product's general manager. As Clark and Fujimoto explain:

> In addition to concept-related duties, the responsibilities that come with the job include: coordinating production and sales as well as engineering; coordinating the entire project from concept to market; signing off on specification, cost-target, layout and major component choices; and maintaining direct contact with existing and potential customers. Heavyweight product managers have a broad knowledge of the product and process engineering required to develop an entire vehicle. Years of experience with the companies give their words weight and increase their influence with people over whom they have no formal authority.

Honda's "large product leader" is such a position. It combines the generation of a strong product concept with the ability to carry it through development to the final product experience for the end-customer.

### Honda Accord: Maintaining Product Integrity

When the product manager for the Honda Accord began the third generation design, he was challenged with maintaining the concept "man maximum, machine minimum" throughout the development process while still repositioning the Accord to fit future customer expectations. Starting with a series of small-group brainstorming sessions, the product leader and his team decided to personify the car's message to consumers with the image of "a rugby player in a business suit." The next step was to break this image down into specific attributes of a car. Five sets of key words were chosen: open-minded; friendly communication; tough spirit; stress-free; and love forever. Tough spirit was translated into maneuverability in difficult conditions. Love forever translated into long-term customer satisfaction. Stress-free led to efforts in noise and vibration reduction.

To capture all of these elements was a challenge for the Accord design team. In an effort to allow maximum space and visibility for the occupants, a low engine hood and a larger-than-usual front window were part of the design. Unfortunately the large window meant that the car could get uncomfortably hot in the summer unless there was a large air conditioner requiring a large engine. And the large engine was contrary to the desire for a low engine hood.

Rather than allowing this to develop into an either-or decision, the product leader reminded the group to look at their work through future customers' eyes and to maintain the integrity of the initial concept. The result was the development of a new engine that was both compact and powerful.

As the Honda example shows, being market-oriented is a critical role of the talented product manager. However, as Clark and Fujimoto also point out, it requires more than that:

> It begins with customers, to be sure, since the best concept developers invariably supplement the cooked information they get from marketing specialists with raw data they gather themselves. But strong product concepts also include a healthy measure of what we call "market imagination": they encompass what customers say they want and what the concept's creators imagine customers will want three or more years into the future. Remembering that customers know only existing products and existing technologies, they avoid the trap of being too close to customers—and of designing products that will be out-of-date before they are even manufactured.

The product manager must juggle numerous details and ensure that the subtleties of a product concept are not lost in the development and marketing. Although creating product and marketing plans is part of this effort, an essential task is the interpersonal communication of the somewhat intangible ideas. Daily communication with functional engineering departments during the design phase and with plant personnel during the development phase is a necessary role of the product manager. Similarly, product managers test-drive the vehicles and continually strive to attain strong product integrity:

> The product manager's job touches every part of the new product process. Indeed, heavyweight product managers have to be "multilingual," fluent in the languages of customers, marketers, engineers, and designers. On one side, this means being able to translate an evocative concept like the pocket rocket into specific targets like "maximum speed 250 kilometers per hour" and

"drag coefficient less than 0.3" that detail-oriented engineers can easily grasp. On the other side, it means being able to assess and communicate what a "0.3 drag coefficient" will mean to the customers.

Outstanding product management organizations depend on the consistency between the formal and informal organizational structure. Honda demonstrated this consistency in some important ways. Communication lines were open and direct rather than indirect. Functional specialists were respected but not put on a pedestal. And the product concept was infused through the product team.

### General Motors: Making Improvements

The lack of a heavyweight product manager can detract from the ability to capture product integrity. When General Motors introduced the Allante in 1987, analysts felt they rushed to introduction rather than working out the bugs. The car was attractive but not necessarily distinctive. It was too small for core Cadillac buyers and lacked the necessary quality to lure import buyers. In other words, it was not externally integrated.

GM's process of product development has been quite different from that of Honda and Chrysler. While those companies place the decisions about a vehicle in the hands of an autonomous team, GM traditionally preferred to preserve the power of functional departments. However, even at GM there has been a shift to a more unified approach. Kathleen Kerwin, in her *Business Week* article, "GM's Aurora," discusses how the development of the Oldsmobile Aurora initiated changes in terms of cross-functional cooperation and increased input from the customer.

[The process of developing the Aurora] meant that the GM design engineers in Flint joined efforts with Oldsmobile's marketing group in Lansing and GM factory managers at the Lake Orion (Mich.) plant. In cases [such as this] where the various teams have a sense of common purpose, the results can be impressive.

At the very least, Aurora is a sign that GM is finally listening to its customers. The No. 1 carmaker had long made a habit of ignoring customer input or delaying market research until the final stages of car development, when it was too late to make changes. By contrast Aurora's development team consulted extensively with consumer focus groups even before the first designs were drawn. Now, the "Voice of the Customer" has become GM's new rallying cry.

Like Ford and Honda, Oldsmobile struggled with product integrity in its work on the Aurora. The vehicle was designed as a niche car, intended to attract affluent, quality-conscious baby boomers. In discussing the car with potential customers, a nameless characteristic kept emerging as an important feature: something about German cars that connoted security and that protected drivers from bumps and jolts. The design team determined this came from a rigid body structure. Unfortunately, providing this rigidity without sacrificing the smooth, flowing lines of the design was a challenge. To accomplish both objectives simultaneously the engineers devised a way to spray molten silicon bronze into the roof seam instead of using conventional welding. The result was a distinctive car that retained the original concept through the design process.

### Product Managers in Other Industries

Heavyweight product managers in other industries have some of the same characteristics as in the automotive industry. As Jean LeGrand states in *Bankers Magazine*, "A Product in Need of Management," a successful product manager in the banking industry "must be a senior-level professional, widely regarded in the profession." This individual must understand "complex portfolio management programs and such quantitative models as cost accounting and ROE computations." And, as in the automotive industry, the position requires market knowledge and the ability to translate technical concepts into customer-appropriate terms.

In fast-moving consumer goods (FMCG) companies, product managers (frequently called brand managers) are less likely to have industry experience, but rather have strong management and marketing skills, typically requiring an MBA. They are expected to create a strong brand recognition for their products through their ability to command respect, maintain momentum throughout a product-related project, and motivate everyone toward the same goal. As with heavyweight product managers in other industries, the FMCG brand manager must strive for and champion product integrity.

Source: Adapted from: Kim B. Clark and Takahiro Fujimoto, "The Power of Product Integrity," *Harvard Business Review* (November-December 1990), 107-118; Christopher Power, "Flops," *Business Week* (16 August, 1993), 76-82; Kathleen Kerwin, "GM's Aurora," *Business Week* (21 March, 1994), 88-95; and Jean E. LeGrand, "A Product in Need of Management," *Banker Magazine* (November-December 1992), 73-76.

# SECTION TWO

# PLANNING SKILLS FOR PRODUCT MANAGERS

One of the primary planning documents or tools that the product manager develops cooperatively with others in the company is the annual marketing plan for the product line. The planning process starts with an examination of current conditions to search for problems and opportunities for the product(s). After the problems and opportunities are identified and synthesized, a statement of direction for the next fiscal year is provided through sales and marketing objectives.

Finally, an action program is established which clarifies the strategies and tactics required to achieve the stated objectives. These strategies and tactics might encompass all of the traditional components of marketing including a refinement of the target market, product changes and/or deletions, modifications in pricing, expansion/contraction or changes among distributors, dealers and retailers, and improvements in marketing communication approaches. Commitment to follow through the strategies and tactics must be obtained from the respective functional areas in the company.

Section Two discusses a process that product managers can use in their annual planning activities and presents a format for the annual product marketing plan.

# 4

# THE PRODUCT MARKETING PLANNING PROCESS

One of the primary expectations of a product manager is the development and execution of an annual product plan to ensure an acceptable sales and profit level for the product or product line in question. The planning process should cover three fundamental questions:

- Where are you now? (Background analysis, Chapter 4)
- Where do you want to go? (Synthesis, Chapter 5)
- How can you get there? (Action program, Chapter 5)

Table 4.1 shows the types of information that make up each part of the process. This chapter covers the fundamental steps involved in the process of planning. The next chapter provides tips on developing a product plan, ending with a sample outline and profit and loss statement.

## Background Analysis: *Where Are You Now?*

The background analysis answers the question, "Where are you now?" and is the analytical part of the planning process that should precede development of the product plan. It includes a business assessment, a market analysis, a competitive analysis, a performance history, and an examination of trend dynamics.

## Business Assessment

The first part of the business assessment is determining the vision and strategy of the overall company. (See Figure 4.1 and Figure 7.1 "Assessing Your Company's Strategic IQ.") The vision is the mental picture of what the company will be in the future: the products it will

**Figure 4.1  Business Assessment: Hierarchy of Strategies**

## Table 4.1  The Product Marketing Planning Process

| Where are you now? | I.  Background Analysis |
|---|---|
|  | Business assessment |
|  | Market analysis |
|  | Competitive analysis |
|  | Performance history |
|  | Trend dynamics |
| Where do you want to go? | II. Synthesis |
|  | Problems & opportunities |
|  | Sales forecasts/goals |
|  | Product objectives |
|  | Positioning strategy |
| How can you get there? | III. Action program |
|  | Summary of background analysis and synthesis |
|  | Target market |
|  | Product strategy |
|  | Pricing strategy |
|  | Advertising strategy |
|  | Promotion strategy |
|  | Field sales strategy |
|  | Distribution strategy |
|  | Product support |
|  | Training requirements |
|  | Marketing research requirements |
|  | Financial summary |
|  | Schedules |

offer and the markets it will serve. The corporate and divisional strategies are the general plans to move toward the vision. The product plans and marketing tactics should be consistent with the vision and strategies and move the company closer to superior customer satisfaction. The vision and corporate strategies are broad, with a focus on developing and leveraging core competencies. The product-specific strategies and tactics focus on customer-specific needs. (See Figure 4.1 and Worksheet 4.1.)

The vision should highlight the core capabilities the company has or is willing to develop. For example, Komatsu, a Japanese manufacturer of earth-moving equipment, had a vision of beating Caterpillar. The strategies specified the skills it needed to acquire and the products it needed to develop to move toward that vision.[1] (See "Komatsu's Long-Term Marketing Challenge.")

The business assessment also looks at the general culture of the company, the strengths that provide the core competence, the weaknesses that must be minimized, and the role a product/line plays in accomplishing the corporate strategy. The culture refers to the way a company operates: its philosophies, management style, and structure. A product manager cannot impact the culture in the short term but must rather understand and attempt to work within the culture. Example philosophies include the innovative, fast-paced organization and the conservative, "blue-chip" organization. The management style could be autocratic or democratic, with a resulting impact on a product manager's effectiveness.

There are several questions to ask as part of the business assessment to help identify key strengths and weaknesses of management, core competencies, the planning process, and other functional areas.

## Management

1. Who are the actual movers and shakers of the company? Which ones should be part of a new-product venture?
2. Who is responsible for the budgeting process?
3. Does the company have any unusual business practices that are different from the competition?

## Core Competencies

1. What capabilities are the core of the firm's reason for being?
2. Are the various products leveraging these competencies effectively? (See Chapter 7 for further discussion.)
3. How can product managers leverage the capabilities of other parts of the company?

## The Planning Process

1. What is the basic approach to tactical and strategic planning?
2. Is it more likely the company will grow by acquisition, penetration of new markets, or increased market share?
3. To what extent are documented objectives used in planning?
4. Where is the emphasis placed for the development of new products (e.g., product line extensions, new applications, new-product ventures, etc.)?
5. What are the plans for global or international growth?
6. What significant new products are under development?

## Komatsu's Long-Term Marketing Challenge

Komatsu, a Japanese manufacturer of bulldozers, developed a strategic vision of being a global player in earthmoving equipment, in essence a vision of beating Caterpillar. This required a series of short-term plans that focused on the immediate problems and opportunities Komatsu had to respond to in the process of achieving its long-term goal.

In the 1960s, Komatsu was about a third the size of Caterpillar, limited to one product line (small bulldozers), and scarcely represented outside of Japan. When Caterpillar threatened Komatsu in Japan, Komatsu's short-term objective was to protect its home market. The strategies used to accomplish this were product improvements, cost reductions, and new product development through licensing agreements. In the early 1970s Komatsu's challenge was to develop export markets. Since it was not yet strong enough to compete head-to-head with Caterpillar, it chose markets where Caterpillar was weak. Then in the late 1970s Komatsu felt prepared to compete against Caterpillar in the U.S. market.

Note how the company started with a long-term vision or direction. Then on a shorter-term basis it focused on the problems and opportunities present at that time (i.e., "Where are we now?"). The corporate challenges represented the synthesis or "Where do we want to go" portion of the marketing planning process. In other words, they focused on the steps that needed to be taken at the current point in

## Komatsu's Short-Term Challenges and Responses

| Date | Corporate Challenge | Activities |
|------|---------------------|------------|
| Early 1960s | Protect Komatsu's home market against Caterpillar | • Licensing deals with Cummins Engine, International Harvester, and Bucyrus-Eric |
| Mid-1960s | Begin quality improvement efforts | • Several quality and cost-reduction programs |
| 1960s to early 1970s | Build export markets | • Komatsu Europe established<br>• Service departments to assist newly industrializing countries |
| Late 1970s | Create new products and markets | • Future and Frontiers program to identify new businesses based on society's needs and company's know-how |

time to move closer to the future picture of the company. Finally, the activities column listed a brief summary of the action program or the tactics necessary to address the corporate challenges (i.e., "How are we going to get there?").

Source: Adapted from Gary Hamel and C. K. Prahalad, "Strategic Intent," *Harvard Business Review* (May-June 1989), 63-76.

---

## *Other Functional Areas*

1. What is the background of the R&D manager?
2. What is the overall caliber of the research staff?
3. What is the company's technical position?
4. Does the company have idle plants and excess capacity?
5. What is the major R&D thrust?
6. How is R&D organized?
7. Is manufacturing productivity increasing or decreasing?

## Worksheet 4.1  Business Assessment

| |
|---|
| 1. Describe the corporate vision, strategies, and core competencies that might affect the product programs. |
| 2. List the strengths and weaknesses of the company that could directly affect the product or product line. <br><br> Strengths: <br><br> Weaknesses: |
| 3. Describe the role your product/line plays in accomplishing the corporate strategy. |

## Market Analysis

Market analysis refers to studying the current and potential customers for a product or product line and then putting them into categories or segments. The segments are groups of customers with common demographics, common needs, and/or common usages for the product. The process of segmenting allows the marketer to get closer to the customer by focusing on the requirements of smaller groups.

It's important to break a total market into submarkets for a variety of reasons. First, it helps provides a better understanding of the aggregate market, including how and why customers buy. Second, it ensures better allocation of resources because the benefits that specific groups are looking for are better understood. This should make it possible to build competitive edges into the product. And, finally, segmentation enables the company to exploit opportunities by uncovering hidden niches.

### Examine and Segment Current Customers

Start with current customers. What is the profile of the average customer? What segment buys the most? The least? What types of customers are most profitable for the firm? Who are the actual buyers and who are the influencers? Are there some segments in the market buying only competitive products? Are there segments that don't yet exist but could be created with a new product?

The next step is to break the overall market down into segments with common needs so that different marketing strategies can be developed for each. For sake of simplicity, let's look at a fictional business product that is sold to three major Standard Industrial Classification (SIC) groups: construction, manufacturing, and services. The three primary needs being addressed by this type of product are speed, ease of use, and optional features. (See Figure 4.2.)

### Figure 4.2 Dominant Needs in Three Market Segments

| | Market Segments | | |
|---|---|---|---|
| Common Needs (Reasons for Buying) | Construction | Manufacturing | Service Sector |
| Speed | 60% | 9% | 12% |
| Ease of use | 20 | 82 | 13 |
| Optional features | 20 | 9 | 75 |

There are three obvious market segments with three dominant needs. The predominant reason the construction segment buys the product is speed; the manufacturing segments buys for ease of use; and the service sector is interested in optional features. By dividing the market into three categories (construction, manufacturing, and services), it's possible to modify the product to address the specific needs, design advertising to communicate the specific benefits to each segment, and possibly compare sales volume in each segment with total industry sales for the product type for each segment.

Figure 4.3 shows a different picture. Note that there is no consistency between industry classification and needs. About a third of each segment desires speed, about a third desires ease of use, and about a third wants optional features. The product manager will need to make a decision here. It would be feasible to focus on a given industry classification and offer that segment three product variations to address the three need preferences. The selection of which industry to target would depend on the size of the segment, its growth rate, the company's current market position in that segment, and the profitability of the segment, as well as other factors.

Another possibility would be to identify in which of the three needs, if any, the product has a competitive edge. If the product is

**Figure 4.3  Inconsistent Needs in Three Market Segments**

| | Market Segments | | |
|---|---|---|---|
| Common Needs (Reasons for Buying) | Construction | Manufacturing | Service Sector |
| Speed | 33% | 33% | 34% |
| Ease of use | 33 | 34 | 33 |
| Optional features | 34 | 33 | 33 |

superior to competitive products in its speed, a needs-based rather than demographics-based segmentation approach will be most successful. In other words, the highest potential market consists of companies requiring speed, regardless of their SIC designation. Therefore, the product manager should determine the percentage of all businesses having speed as a dominant need and focus on that group as the market.

To conduct this type of analysis, use segmentation factors most appropriate for the industry. (See Figure 4.4.) Consumer product companies use demographic variables such as age, family status, or life-style. Industrial product companies use the Standard Industrial Classification (SIC), company size, or functional titles. Service companies use intensity of need, risk categories, or distance from the company. Many companies use end-use of the product as a segmentation variable. For example, a product manager for nylon might break segments into end-use groups such as menswear, tires, and upholstery.

### Determine the Importance and Profitability of Each Segment to the Firm

After identifying segments that have different needs, examine the product's performance in each segment. What is the average order size, the share of segment sales, and the revenue generated? The example in Figure 4.5 shows four identifiable market segments. Segment A consists of the largest companies with special demands and the market power to negotiate for those demands. In rating the importance of six purchase criteria on a scale of 1 to 5 with 1 being "low importance" and 5 being "essential," price has an importance level of 4, quality/features is rated 1, delivery 3, installation 1, man-

**Figure 4.4  Segmentation Factors**

| | Product-Market | |
|---|---|---|
| Type of Factor | Consumer | Business-to-Business |
| Demographic | Age, sex, race<br>Income<br>Family size<br>Family life-cycle<br>　stage<br>Location<br>Life-style | Industry (SIC)<br>Geographic location<br>Company size<br>Functional<br>　decision maker<br>Profitability<br>Risk categories |
| Application/<br>use of product | Frequency of purchase<br>Size of purchase<br>How product is used | Application<br>Importance of<br>　purchase<br>Volume<br>Frequency of purchase |
| Benefits<br>(possibly<br>beyond the<br>product itself) | Desired benefits of<br>　product<br>Psychological benefits<br>Service<br>Intensity of need | Performance<br>　requirements<br>Support service<br>Desired features<br>Service requirements |

ufacturing/engineering support 1, and sales coverage 2. Based on industry data, the company estimates the overall sales in the segment are $89 million with an average order size of $15,000. Its share of this market is 13 percent, with an average order size of $1,500. By studying this information, it appears that the company is most successful with Segments B and C.

## Figure 4.5  Segmentation by Key Buying Factors

| | Segment A | Segment B | Segment C | Segment D |
|---|---|---|---|---|
| **Common purchase decision criteria** | ■ "Category killers"<br>■ Standard products<br>■ Large purchases<br>■ Strong price negotiators | ■ Large customers<br>■ Very price-sensitive<br>■ Standard products<br>■ Large purchases | ■ Medium-size customers<br>■ Modified standard products<br>■ Medium-size lots<br>■ Fairly price-sensitive | ■ Any size customer<br>■ Nonstandard motors<br>■ Small lots<br>■ Price often secondary |
| **Price** | | | | |
| **Quality/features** | | | | |
| **Delivery** | | | | |
| **Installation** | | | | |
| **Marketing/ engineering support** | | | | |
| **Sales coverage** | | | | |
| **Size and share** | $89 million<br>13% | $113.4 million<br>31% | $69.3 million<br>30% | $66.6 million<br>25% |
| **Average order size** | $1,500<br>Industry: $15,000 | $6,998<br>Industry: $5,000 | $2,345<br>Industry: $2,000 | $923<br>Industry: $1,100 |

Key to importance of buying factors

| 1 | 2 | 3 | 4 | 5 |
|---|---|---|---|---|

Least important                                                                 Most important

## *Carefully Evaluate Each Segment for Changes that Might Affect Attractiveness or Strategy*

Using secondary data, estimate the size of the segments in the overall market. Multiply by average revenue per customer to determine total revenue potential (for all competitors in the industry).

Attractiveness can be determined by the absolute size of the segment, its growth rate, the strength of competition in that segment, or a variety of other factors appropriate in the industry. Compare the size, purchase volumes, and growth rate for the segments in the total market with the size, purchase volumes, and growth rate of the segments in a specific customer base. Ask questions during this analysis. What is the demand in each segment for the product? What is the product's penetration? How many prospects are there in segments that purchase only competitive products? Why do they? Are you gaining or losing share? Do you participate in the most profitable segments of the industry?

Also, look for changes that could affect the product or its marketing strategy. Hartford Insurance, for example, found that the fabricated metals industry was beginning to export to foreign markets. As a result, it developed expanded international coverage to serve this segment.[2]

### Look for New Segments that Are Highly Profitable or Are Underserved by Competitors

This step forces a product manager to look beyond the current customer base to look for opportunities. There are almost always customer groups that are not being reached effectively but that present potential opportunities for a firm. Markets are becoming increasingly fragmented, so they must be analyzed in that way. For example, the small-office, home-office (SOHO) market has grown dramatically in the past decade, providing segmentation opportunities to a variety of firms from banks to office products to telecommunications. At the opposite end of the spectrum, "category killers" such as Wal-Mart and Home Depot have become segments for many manufacturers, fueling the growth of national account programs.

Start with informal research among current customers. Try to find unusual uses or applications for the product to determine whether these could be developed into product-market segments. Conduct research among competitors' customers to determine level of satisfaction, perceived strengths and weaknesses, and areas of unmet needs. Examine sources of influence, the budgeting process, seasonality, and other aspects of the process of buying to try to uncover different need segments. Look at where the market buys to determine whether different segments can be developed from different distribution channels. And don't overlook the possibility of segments that could be created by developing new products.

### Prioritize the Old and New Segments

After listing potential ways of segmenting the market, including both old and new market segments, the next step is to reduce the number of categories into a manageable number (3-7). First, eliminate any segments that the firm cannot serve, for whatever reason. Then examine the remaining segments in terms of fit with company resources, fit with long-term strategy, cost to reach, and risk to serve. Rank these segments so that the greatest proportion of resources will be devoted to the most important segments and the lowest proportion of resources to the least important segments. Adapt the example in Figure 4.5 to complete Worksheet 4.2 (Market Analysis).

## Competitive Analysis

The competitive analysis is a summary of what might be pages (or even files) of information compiled from published and internal sources. Annual reports, newspaper articles, trade shows, salespeople, government and trade association reports, and informal conversa-

## Worksheet 4.2  Market Analysis

| Needs (reasons for buying) | Market Segments | | | | |
|---|---|---|---|---|---|
| | | | | | |
| | | | | | |
| | | | | | |
| | | | | | |
| | | | | | |
| Size and share | | | | | |
| Average order size | | | | | |
| Segment rank | | | | | |

tions with customers can provide much of the necessary information. However, to analyze customer perceptions of the competitive strengths and weaknesses, some type of marketing research will be necessary. (See Worksheet 4.3.)

Competitive intelligence is an important part of a product manager's job. Part of the responsibility is to understand a product's competition so that threats can be minimized. Start with the most easily obtained data, including published information. Financial reports, published price lists, competitive ads and promotional materials, product spec sheets, and trade articles can provide a wealth of information if analyzed. The financial reports can provide clues about future strategies; the ads can suggest how the competitor is positioning the product; and the specification sheets can help in benchmarking.

If the competition is a privately held company or a division of a larger company, subscribe to the hometown newspaper where the product is manufactured. Or subscribe to an on-line search service to monitor the main competitor.

In analyzing information, do not stop with the current, static data. Look at the data over time to study trends and changes that might help develop assumptions about competitive marketing strategies. Identifying possible competitive marketing strategies provides the information necessary to predict future actions or reactions to tactical maneuvers.

## Competitors and Competing Products

1. To which competitors have you lost business and from which have you gained business? (This is the competition from the customer's perspective.)
2. Where (in what regions, applications, industries, etc.) is competition the strongest? Why?
3. What are the corporate competencies of the companies that own competing products? What is the relationship between the competencies and the products?

4. What are the list prices of the competing products? The actual prices?

5. What is the market perception of the competing products? Awareness level? Customer loyalty?

6. Are there any specific product features that are "best-in-class," against which your product should be benchmarked?

7. Is the competing product a small percentage of its company's business, or is it *the* product of the company? How important are the sales to the competitor, and how much is the company willing to invest to protect these sales?

## Performance History

The performance history looks at how well a product performed over time and relative to plan. It focuses attention on the market share and financial and other numeric or statistical indicators of performance. In addition, answers to product mix questions like the ones listed below provide qualitative data that could highlight problems and opportunities to be addressed in the marketing plan. (See Worksheet 4.4.)

### Existing Customers

1. Is there a group of heavy users of the product(s)? What percentage of the purchasers do they constitute?

2. Is the primary target market growing, stable, or declining?

3. Under what circumstances do customers purchase the product(s)?

4. How and why is geographical coverage limited?

## Worksheet 4.3  Competitive Analysis

### General Information for 19__

| Division: | Group: | Product Line: | Market: |
|---|---|---|---|

|  | Your Product | Product A | Product B | Product C | Product D |
|---|---|---|---|---|---|
| Sales volume (units) | | | | | |
| Sales revenue ($) | | | | | |
| Profit | | | | | |
| Market share | | | | | |
| Target market(s) | | | | | |
| General product strategy | | | | | |
| Product differentiation | | | | | |
| Customer image | | | | | |
| General price strategy | | | | | |
| Average/list price | | | | | |
| General pro- motion strategy | | | | | |
| General distri- bution strategy | | | | | |
| Sales force size | | | | | |
| Sales force strengths: | | | | | |

5. What percentage of customers are national accounts? International?
6. Are most customers new or repeat buyers?
7. Are the customers the end-users? If not, what information is available about the end-user?
8. Are your customers progressive? Traditional? Passive?
9. How sensitive have customers been to past price changes?
10. Does the customer base consist of a few large customers or many small buyers?

## The Product

1. What does the name of the product imply? Can it be branded?
2. Which of the features are distinguishable by the customer?
3. For each feature, ask "So what?" to identify the benefits from the customer's point of view.
4. Is the product supplied through intermediaries (e.g., dealers)? If so, the analysis of features/benefits should be handled in two steps.
5. If a numeric rating were given to the product quality (with 1 being low and 7 being high), what would that rating be? Would the rating be the same from the customers?
6. What does each item in the product line contribute to sales and profits? To customer satisfaction? Can some of the products be pruned?
7. How does the product line rate of return compare with the company's overall rate of return?
8. Is the product design conducive to an efficient manufacturing process?

9. What are the engineering costs for product development, product engineering, and manufacturing engineering?
10. What is the unit break-even sales for the product?
11. Are product guarantees competitive?
12. What would happen if the products were more standardized? More customized?
13. What is the company's attitude toward private labeling?

## The Sales Force

1. Is the current sales force structure appropriate for achieving the product objectives?
2. Are the target customers being reached in the most effective manner?
3. How effective has the product/sales training been?
4. What sales tools do the salespeople actually use to sell the product?
5. Has the sales force been taught how to help customers visualize the benefits of the product?

## Pricing

1. Have significant amounts of business been lost because of product prices?
2. Are errors frequently made in pricing?
3. What is the perceived cost of buying the product/service?
4. Is the company a price leader or a price follower?
5. What is the pricing policy of the company?
6. What types of discounts are offered? How does that compare with the competition?

## Worksheet 4.4 Performance History

| Division: | Group: | | Product Line: | | Market: | |
|---|---|---|---|---|---|---|
| | | **19__** | | **19__** | | **19__** |
| | | Plan | Actual | Plan | Actual | Plan | Actual |
| Industry volume (units) | | | | | | | |
| Your volume | | | | | | | |
| Percentage of industry volume | | | | | | | |
| Industry sales ($) | | | | | | | |
| Your sales | | | | | | | |
| Percentage of industry sales | | | | | | | |
| Product sales as percentage of company sales | | | | | | | |
| Cost of goods sold | | | | | | | |
| Gross margin | | | | | | | |
| Gross margin ratio | | | | | | | |
| Controllable costs | | | | | | | |
| Promotion | | | | | | | |
| Field sales costs | | | | | | | |
| Other marketing costs | | | | | | | |
| Misc. controllable costs | | | | | | | |
| Total controllable costs | | | | | | | |
| Net profit contribution | | | | | | | |
| Quality index | | | | | | | |
| New product sales | | | | | | | |
| Target account sales | | | | | | | |
| Price index | | | | | | | |
| Sales per salesperson | | | | | | | |
| Product/line strengths | | | | | | | |
| Product/line weaknesses | | | | | | | |

### The Promotional Campaigns

1. What is the current image customers have of the product? Is it consistent with the advertising?
2. Did prior advertising strategies work? Why or why not?
3. What non-advertising promotion has been tried? How well did it work?

### The Distribution Strategy

1. What is the company's relationship with intermediaries (e.g., distributors, agents, retailers, etc.)?
2. What are the channels of distribution? What percentage of the product sales are through each type of intermediary?
3. What are distribution costs as a percentage of sales?
4. How does the company's policy for distributor/retailer margins compare with those of the competition?
5. What has been the recent history of stock-outs, substitutes, and back-orders?

### Support Services

1. Has the value of repair services changed (due to cost increases, repair person efficiency, or any other reason)?

## Trend Dynamics

An examination of trends and their dynamics relative to a product's success is the final part of the background analysis. External trends have a direct bearing on market potential even though they are a less tangible part of the analysis. In answering the following questions, select major events that are likely to affect the company, the competitors, the product, and markets served by the company.

1. What technological changes are likely? How might they impact product sales within the next several years?
2. What have been the industry trends in terms of the following:

   - Product changes
   - Price levels/policies
   - Distribution changes
   - Mergers/acquisitions/divestitures
   - Power shifts in the channel

3. What leading indicators correspond with product sales?
4. What are the basic trends and changes in the economy?
5. Are there regulatory or political forces that could impact product sales? What are their trends?
6. What is the probability of the above trends occurring?
7. What impact do these have on the product(s)?

## References

1. Gary Hamel and C. K. Prahalad, "Strategic Intent," *Harvard Business Review* 67 (May/June 1989): 63-76.

2. Marian B. Wood and Evelyn Ehrlich, "Segmentation: Five Steps to More Effective Business Marketing," *Sales & Marketing Management* 143 (April 1991): 59.

## Checklist: The Product Marketing Planning Process

✓ Start the annual planning process by carefully assessing the current status of your product and your company. Look for problems to address during the next fiscal year as well as opportunities to exploit.

✓ Break your customers into groups or segments that allow you to allocate your resources most effectively and provide you the greatest competitive opportunities. Don't be afraid to think about your customers in new ways.

✓ Begin your competitive analysis by asking yourself to whom have you lost the most business or from whom have you gained the most business. Don't limit your analysis to only the top companies in the industry.

✓ Study the performance of your product(s) over a three-year period. Look at the stability of the customers for each product, the effectiveness of prices and price changes, the sales and profit trends by product, the attitude of the sales force, and any other variables which could explain differences in performance.

✓ Try to predict the effect current trends will have on the future of your product. Are regulatory forces likely to require design changes? Are there indications customers are shifting in preference toward competing technologies? Whenever possible, prepare for the potential changes before you are forced to.

# 5

# THE ANNUAL PRODUCT PLAN

## Synthesis: Where Do You Want to Go?

The synthesis is the section of the annual product plan that ties together the background analysis with the vision by indicating what steps will be taken this fiscal year to move closer to the future picture of the company's product line. This will include the forecast of sales volume, the marketing objectives that specify the market segments from which the volume will be generated, and the positioning of the product in the customers' minds.

### Problems and Opportunities

After examining the background as described in Chapter 4, the next step is to synthesize the information to look for problems or opportunities and decide where to go from there. Problems or opportunities are the conclusions drawn and can arise from any part of the background analysis. For example, the analysis might uncover new niches that previously had been overlooked, a declining market share that was camouflaged by a growing market segment, or an inconsistent product image. In any case, focus on problems to correct or opportunities to exploit in the product marketing plan. Without this step of drawing conclusions, the background analysis is often perceived as a waste of time and is not made relevant to the marketing plan.

## Hewlett-Packard: Problems and Opportunities for the Deskjet

Hewlett-Packard introduced the Deskjet in 1988. Sales came slowly. By 1989 the product wasn't meeting its sales goals, even though there was an absence of strong competition. An analysis determined that the Deskjet was taking business away from H-P's own laser printers, rather than the competition, resulting in a lower profit margin per sale.

After identifying the problem, H-P decided to reposition the Deskjet as a competitor to dot-matrix printers instead of as a lower-cost alternative to laser printers. To attain this objective, H-P started by thoroughly studying Epson, the leader in the industry. The company began to track Epson's market share. It evaluated Epson's marketing practices, profiled its top managers, and surveyed its customers. Engineers tore apart Epson printers to better understand the technology used. H-P discovered that Epson printers were placed in prominent spots in stores, customers perceived the printers as reliable, and the products were designed for easy manufacturability.

Armed with this information, Hewlett-Packard planned the actions that were necessary to reposition the Deskjet. First, the company convinced stores to place Deskjets next to the Epson dot-matrix printers to emphasize the competitive positioning. Second, H-P extended its warranty to three years to assure buyers that the Deskjet was reliable. And finally, the inkjets were redesigned with manufacturability in mind.

Source: Adapted from Stephen Kreider Yoder, "How H-P Used Tactics of the Japanese to Beat Them at Their Game," *Wall Street Journal,* September 8, 1994, 1+.

---

Setting marketing and sales objectives follows the identification of problems and opportunities. Frequently a product manager is given a financial sales goal, and his or her job is to design a marketing program to make it happen. In other cases, the product manager must present the sales forecast to management with a justification or rationale. Typically there is some combination of the two approaches.

### Sales Forecasting

The product manager will be responsible for forecasting product sales or, at a minimum, understanding the forecasts received. There are three categories of forecasting techniques that might be used:

1. **Time series forecasts** can be obtained from historical data on past product sales to project into the future for short-term sales figures.
2. **Compiled forecasts,** as the term implies, are compilations of data from qualitative and quantitative research.
3. **Causal forecasts** are derived from relating sales to the factors that cause the sales to happen.

Although a product manager usually works with an analyst to obtain these figures, it is important to understand the basic ramifications of the three categories of forecasts.

**Time Series**  A logical place to start forecasting future sales is to look at historical sales patterns. Time series analyses look at changes in sales over time. Plotting a product's sales over time gives the product manager a picture of the product's sales trends. Trend-fitting, or regression, plots the sales over time and uses a statistical formula to fit a line through the data points and then project that line into the future. Trend-fitting is relatively simple and fast to do by computer and is easy to understand. It can be accurate in the short term if there are no external factors that make the future sales environment significantly different from the past sales environment.

There are several averages that are time series based. A moving average forecasts sales using X time periods from the past (e.g., the average of the past 12 months' data). Each data point has the same weight unless seasonal indexes or other weights are built in. As the average moves into the future, it drops off the oldest data point from the calculations. Exponential smoothing is a form of moving average that provides heavier weights to the most recent data. This is done because it is assumed that recent data are more valuable in predicting future sales than older data.

Box-Jenkins is a more sophisticated version of exponential smoothing. This technique uses a computer to test different time series models for the best fit. For example, the number of data points as well as the different weights affect the time series line, so it is important to track how effective the various techniques were in providing a mathematical line close to the actual line of sales points.

Time series techniques are appropriate when the sales environment does not change and when the effectiveness of a marketing plan has no impact on sales. Generally, neither of these is true. As a result, marketing research information and/or causal information should be part of the forecasting process.

**Compiled Forecasts** The marketing research used for forecasting can be a combination of compiling secondary and primary data as well as qualitative and quantitative approaches to data collection. Some of the secondary data can be pulled from the product fact book. Worksheet 4.4. in Chapter 4 provides information on industry/category sales for a product/line. Look at average market share over time and multiply this average by the projected industry sales for the next fiscal year. The result is an approximate sales forecast based on the industry projection. Adjust this forecast using qualitative information on trends or other elements that could influence product sales.

In terms of primary data collection, both qualitative and quantitative inputs are important. Quantitative input can come from frontline sources. Salespeople provide estimates by account or territory and regional managers provide estimates by distributor or channel type. An example sales force form is shown in Figure 5.1. In the

## Figure 5.1 Sales Force Customer Analysis Form

| Account | Product A | | Product B | | Product C | |
|---|---|---|---|---|---|---|
| | Sales | Probability | Sales | Probability | Sales | Probability |
| Vaporware | $1,000 | .60 | $600 | .60 | $400 | .60 |
| Tunnel Vision | 2,000 | .50 | 700 | .80 | 700 | .60 |
| Virus-Aid | 1,500 | .70 | 900 | .75 | 300 | .90 |
| Data-Notes | 1,000 | .50 | 600 | .96 | 600 | .80 |

example, the salespeople are asked to estimate sales for each major account for selected products, with their best estimate of the probability of closing the sale during the upcoming quarter. The form can be adapted to include volume rather than dollar revenue, annual rather than quarterly estimates, or other industry-specific variables. The product manager (or analyst) can calculate the expected values by multiplying the sales estimates for each product by the relevant probabilities. In the example, the expected sales of Product A for this particular salesperson would be $3,150 (the sum of the sales times the probability for each account). Customers can also be surveyed directly to assess their probable purchases by product or for the entire line.

Qualitative forecasting techniques are also useful, particularly for new products. Concept testing, in conjunction with intent-to-buy surveys, can be a data point for the new product forecast. Other tools include the Delphi technique and trade data. (See Chapter 8.)

**Causal or Correlation-Based Forecasts** Causal techniques attempt to find relationships between sales and other variables. For example, tire sales are related to vehicular sales, and sales of many household products are related to housing starts. If there are leading indicators (such as vehicle sales or housing starts) that can be used to better understand the sales environment for a product, they should be used in the forecasting process. Sales can also be affected by advertising expenditures, number of salespeople, price changes, or other marketing variables. If a causal relationship between a change in marketing expenditures and a change in sales can be demonstrated, that information can be used not only in forecasting, but also as justification for spending a given amount in the marketing plan.

The forecasted sales figures used in a marketing plan should be based on a variety of inputs. Do not rely exclusively on trend projections, and do not accept upper management's sales forecasts without question. Try to reconcile the unit and dollar amounts based on the background analysis and the anticipated marketing plan/budget.

## *Objectives and Strategies*

The next step is to develop objectives and strategies. The objectives answer the question, "What do you want to happen?" or "What do you need to do to reach the sales forecast?" The strategy states the "how" of the objectives. The objectives should be stated in numeric format whenever possible so that they are measurable. Objectives can be in terms of units or dollars (revenue and/or margin), market share, customer satisfaction level, etc. The objective starts with a verb (increase, maintain, solidify, etc.), acting on a specific goal (repeat purchases, new trial, sales volume/revenue, etc.) for a stated market (existing customers, new customers, or an identified market segment) within a specified time (during the last quarter, within the next 12 months, etc.) An example objective would be as follows:

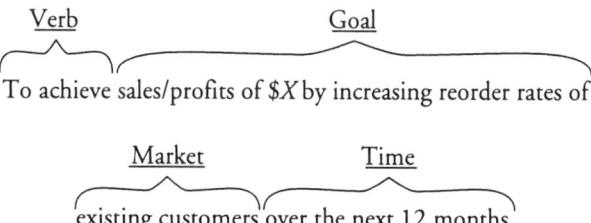

Justify the objectives by providing rationale from the prior worksheets. For example, if the background analysis uncovered the fact that reorder rates are declining even though customer satisfaction is high and there are no obvious problems, it could be argued that the objective can be obtained if appropriate support is provided.

Generally, there will be a general marketing objective, followed by specific objective and strategy statements for each element of the marketing mix (as appropriate for a firm). Always make sure that the entire plan is coordinated so that it has maximum effectiveness.

## *Positioning*

The next part of the synthesis phase is positioning—deciding how a product is to be perceived in the minds of the customer, relative to the competition. Imagine talking to a customer who asks, "Why should I buy from you?" What should the answer be? What makes your product a better buy than competitive products? In this analysis, consider the customer's frame of reference (i.e., the products they would consider likely competitors). Different customers will have different frames of reference that would require different positionings. Therefore, the positioning statement should identify the relevant market segment, that segment's frame of reference, the product's point of differentiation, and an indication of why a product provides that differentiation (i.e., the internal strength of competitive edge that makes a claim of differentiation credible). An example positioning statement might be the following:

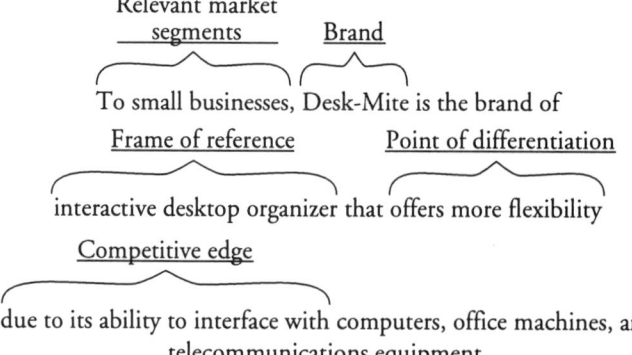

Relevant market
segments            Brand

To small businesses, Desk-Mite is the brand of

Frame of reference        Point of differentiation

interactive desktop organizer that offers more flexibility

Competitive edge

due to its ability to interface with computers, office machines, and
telecommunications equipment.

## The Importance of Customer Retention as a Marketing Objective

Companies are realizing that customer retention is as important, if not more important, than getting new customers. According to *Business Marketing* magazine:

> An October 1994 study by Marketing Metrics showed that of the 165 companies surveyed, respondents, on average, allocate 53% of marketing budgets to retain existing customers and 47% to win new customers. A similar 1991 study showed 46% of marketing budgets went to retention, while 54% went to acquiring new customers.

Cellular One of New York and New Jersey, for example, has part of its marketing department devoted solely to customer retention. Some of the tactics include a 24-hour Customer Care Center and a Corporate Care Center for special corporate accounts. David Straus, director of customer base marketing, says, "Our job really starts once the customer is in the door."

New York-based Bowne & Co., one of the world's largest financial printers, publishes a customer newsletter as a tool in customer retention. By keeping customers abreast of changes in their industries, Bowne & Co. is better able to differentiate itself from other financial service providers.

Source: Adapted from Kim Cleland, "Firms Want Customers Coming Back for More," *Business Marketing* (January 1995), 4+.

Start by identifying the attributes customers are looking for when they buy from the product category, and find out how important each attribute is. Is delivery important? How about minimum tolerances? How important? Next, have customers rate the product in question versus the competition along all the important attributes. Try to isolate attributes for which customers already believe the product is competitively superior *and* that the company can protect using its core abilities, knowledge, or other strength. If this cannot be found, the job of the product manager is to determine how to build it into the product. (See Worksheet 5.1.)

## Worksheet 5.1  Marketing Objectives and Strategies

| Division: | Group: | Product Line: | Market: |
|---|---|---|---|

**General marketing objective(s):**

**Rationale for objectives:**

**Positioning statement:**

To _____ , _____ is the brand of

       (Market segment)            (Your product name)

_____ that _____

       (Frame of reference)            (Point of differentiation)

due to _____

          (Competitive edge)

## The Action Program: How Are We Going to Get There?

The purpose of the annual product marketing plan is to provide top management with a concise marketing and financial summary of objectives and strategies along with the requirements to achieve the objectives. There should be enough rationale to allow them to approve the necessary expenditures without the detail available in a product fact book. Keep the plan as brief as possible, perhaps no more than six or eight pages (excluding charts and exhibits). Too much detail obscures the main issues involved.

On the other hand, do not use the desire for brevity as an excuse for not collecting information. If some information needed to support a recommendation is not available, mention it in the plan (at least as a footnote) to demonstrate that critical data are not being ignored, but that there is sufficient confidence with the other information to justify taking the risk.

If the product plan is to be presented orally as part of a meeting, be sure to come prepared to answer any questions that might arise. Nothing is more frustrating to top management than to reschedule a meeting or make it longer than necessary because of a product manager's lack of preparation.

The written plan consists of a summary of the product's historical performance, a statement of problems and opportunities, sales forecasts/goals and a summary table of the impact on profit and loss (P&L), marketing objectives for the product or product line, concise strategies for accomplishing the objectives, and a series of financial and other exhibits to permit a quick assessment of the product program and its impact.

Separate strategy documents might need to be prepared for operational use as a product manager. Simply provide a concise summary of each as part of the annual product plan, perhaps in the format of listing the objective(s) for that element of the program and providing a brief overview of the strategy to accomplish that objective. Be careful, however, that the complete plan is coordinated. Do not work on the advertising strategy document, for example, without coordinating it with the other elements of the marketing mix.

There are several possible formats for a written product plan; there is no one best approach. Figure 5.2 is only an example. Modify it as appropriate for a given product line, company, and circumstances. The format of objectives/strategies for the various marketing components is quite typical for a written plan, with rationale or justification included.

## Figure 5.2 Marketing Plan Outline

| Topic Outline | Description |
| --- | --- |
| **Product performance** | 2-3 paragraphs summarizing the product's performance relative to last year's plan, along with explanations of variances from plan. Any research conducted on product performance or quality can be included in this section as well. |
| **Background** | Highlights from the background analysis, using bullet points as much as possible. It is useful to include the market analysis, competitive analysis, and/or performance history worksheets as attachments or exhibits. |

| Topic Outline | Description |
|---|---|
| **Problems/opportunities** | |
| 1. Problems | Problems that might make it difficult to achieve the objectives. List the steps to be taken to minimize the risk. |
| 2. Opportunities | Opportunities that will help in achieving the objectives. |
| **Sales forecasts/goals** | A statement of the product's forecasted sales for the next fiscal year. If there are several products or product lines to be examined separately, use a tabular format. |
| **Marketing objectives** | Brief statements of objectives for the product or line for the next fiscal year. These can be stated in terms of revenue/profit, new-product trials, retention rates, etc. |
| **Marketing program** | |
| 1. Positioning statement | The positioning statement from Worksheet 5.1. Make sure that it lists the unique selling feature(s) of the product (i.e., how the product is to be perceived in the customer's mind relative to the competition). The positioning statement should be clear enough to be the "glue" for coordinating the subsequent marketing mix variables. |
| 2. Target market(s) | Several paragraphs with a description of and rationale for the primary and secondary target markets. |

| Topic Outline | Description |
|---|---|
| 3. Product strategy | This section can contain several items, depending on the company and product requirements. There will be one or more objectives, each followed by a brief strategy statement. The format will usually be as follows:<br>■ **Brief product description** (such as might be contained in a catalog) indicating the competitive differences, along with a table of the sizes and variety of products in the line.<br>■ **Product objectives,** including new uses, repositioning, line extensions/modifications, programs to improve quality, or new-product introductions.<br>■ **Objective(s)**<br>■ **Strategy**<br>■ **Rationale**<br>■ **Capacity utilization,** including existing capacity along with manufacturing requirements of the marketing plan. |
| 4. Pricing strategy | A general statement of the pricing strategy used for the product(s). Include any planned changes in price, discounts, warranties, and terms and conditions of sale, along with a table indicating the expected impact on selling and profit performance. The format will be as follows: |

| Topic Outline | Description |
|---|---|

- **Brief description**
- **Objective**
- **Strategy**
- **Rationale**
- **Impact table**

5. Advertising strategy
  a. National
     advertising

This section will have three components:

1. The competitive product differentiation to include in the advertising message
2. The media plan along with a calendar of expected insertions
3. Cost/spending information
   - Brief description
   - Objective
   - Strategy
   - Rationale
   - Implementation
   - Supporting tables

  b. Cooperative
     advertising

A statement of the goals and general program description of cooperative advertising programs with channel members.

  c. Trade advertising If advertising to intermediaries who resell the product, the message and media plan should be summarized in this section.

6. Promotion strategy There are several types of sales promotion, support materials, trade show plans, and

| Topic Outline | Description |
| --- | --- |
| | other non-advertising promotions that may be part of the marketing plan. These may be part of separate plans or strategy documents but should at least be summarized in this section. The format should be consistent with the others:<br>■ Objective<br>■ Strategy |
| 7. Field sales plan | The field sales plan is almost always a separate planning document. Nevertheless, include any information that directly impacts the product or its marketing plan. For example, any training or incentive programs that are part of the budget or that are recommended in addition to the standard field sales plan should be included here. |
| 8. Distribution strategy | Any recommendations regarding changes to the channel of distribution, including adding or deleting intermediaries, should be included. Also incorporate any programs necessary to motivate channel members or to collect information about the end user from them. The format is as follows:<br>■ Objective<br>■ Strategy |
| 9. Product support | Any recommendations regarding the warranty/guarantee for the product, customer service changes, or any other product support issues that affect the achievement of |

| Topic Outline | Description |
| --- | --- |
| | the product objectives. Maintain the format used earlier, such as the following:<br>■ Objective<br>■ Strategy |
| **Training requirements** | Any training requirements (e.g., for customers) not included elsewhere in the marketing plan. |
| **Marketing research requirements** | Any planned research for the fiscal year, providing the proposal as an attachment. |
| **Financial summary** | A pro forma profit and loss statement for the product(s). (See Figure 5.3.) |
| **Schedules** | An action schedule indicating who does what by when. Allow space for the appropriate individuals to sign and date their agreement to the stated tasks. |

## *Target Market*

The first part of the action plan is the description of the target market. There will very likely be a primary target market as well as secondary targets developed from the market analysis in Chapter 4 (Worksheet 4.2). The segments the product manager elects to target determine the marketing strategy as well as the product positioning and communication approaches. For example, Marvin Windows isolated different needs among different segments of window buyers and advanced its position from eighth to third in the industry by stressing the most relevant benefits to each group. (See "Segmentation at Marvin Windows.")

Part of the target market decision will also include the marshalling of resources to get the greatest impact for the marketing

## Figure 5.3  Profit and Loss Statement

| | Previous Year | Percent Sales | Current Year | Percent Sales | Next Year | Percent Sales |
|---|---|---|---|---|---|---|
| Product sales revenue | $ | | $ | | $ | |
| Less price adjustments | | | | | | |
| Cost of goods | — | | — | | — | |
| Gross margin | | % | | % | | % |
| Controllable marketing expenses | | | | | | |
| Advertising | | | | | | |
| Trade allowances | | | | | | |
| Promotions | | | | | | |
| Trade shows | | | | | | |
| Sales support | | | | | | |
| Training | | | | | | |
| Total controllable marketing expenses | — | | — | | — | |
| Product manager contribution margin | | % | | % | | % |
| Other product expenses | | | | | | |
| Sales force cost | | | | | | |
| Distribution | | | | | | |
| Administration | | | | | | |
| Miscellaneous | — | | — | | — | |
| Total other product expenses | | % | | % | | % |
| Total expenses | — | | — | | — | |
| Product contribution to overhead | | % | | % | | % |
| Increase/decrease | % | | % | | % | |

## Segmentation at Marvin Windows

Marvin, a family-owned and controlled window manufacturer in Warroad, Minnesota, discovered the value of market segmentation in reaching its customers more effectively. By studying buying processes it identified builders, dealers, remodelers, and architects as influence groups and designed segment-specific advertising messages to reach them. For example, remodelers want windows that fit existing openings and don't require "customizing" the wall to fit a standard window. For this group, Marvin positioned itself as *the* made-to-order window manufacturer. In reaching building supply dealers, Marvin focused on a lowered need for inventory, thereby increasing dealer profitability. For builders and architects, Marvin emphasized its ability to meet both aesthetic and budgetary constraints.

Source: Adapted from Kate Bertrand, "Divide and Conquer," *Business Marketing* 74 (October 1989): 49-50.

investment and to accomplish an objective such as being an industry leader. Industry leadership in the past meant being the biggest and having the most visible brands. Now, with markets fragmenting, leadership can be defined with a niche concept. By focusing a firm's resources on smaller segments, the firm becomes more visible and gains a perception of leadership in that segment.

The most important insight . . . is the degree to which this whole concept validates the merits of a "niche" or "focus" strategy — seeking to become a large fish in a small pond. A brand of ice cream or beer carried in 500 retail outlets will benefit disproportionately . . . if all those outlets are in Iowa, not spread over the Midwest, and even more if they are in Des Moines. A business-to-business marketer can achieve the same level of visibility and "leadership position" by focusing on one industry. Becoming the leading supplier of inventory software for meatpackers may be not only a feasible objective, but one that confers all the "snowball" benefits of brand leadership within that industry.[1]

## Product Strategy

Several objectives in the product plan are necessary to accomplish a stated sales forecast. For example, a product objective could be to attain sales of $X for each of three major products. The supporting strategy would explain what modifications this would require in terms of quality improvements, "bundling," or new uses. The rationale would explain why this is possible given the background analysis.

Branding and packaging might or might not be a crucial part of the plan, but they should at least be considered. Be sure that the customer need is addressed and explain why a specific product satisfies this need better than the competition. Also, mention the effect of other products on the product line and/or the effect of the line on the company product mix.

New-product plans might be separate because they usually cover a different time period from the annual plan. However, because they impact a product manager's bottom line, they should probably be summarized here. New-product specifications, positioning, budget, and event schedules can be included. (See Section 3 for more information on product strategies and tactics.)

## Pricing Strategy

The pricing section should start with a statement of general company policies and how specific product pricing fits within those policies. Any changes in discounts, price packages, warranties, terms and conditions of sale, or any other variables should be listed, along with an explanation of the impact on the profitability of the line and of the "fit" in the overall positioning and product strategy. (See Chapter 9 for more information on pricing.)

## Advertising Strategy

The advertising section could be the longest if several types of advertising are used. The national (or regional) advertising directed at the end customer will require a different message and media than does advertising directed at the trade. Therefore, separate campaigns will need to be developed. In any case, the product manager must make sure the media and messages are coordinated to match the positioning statement and overall marketing objectives stated in the annual plan.

The media planning part of the strategy should list the media vehicles used to convey the message in a calendar format. (See Figure 5.4.) The rationale should explain why this mix of media and insertions will accomplish the reach/frequency/cost goals of the campaign. (See Chapter 10 for more information on advertising.)

## Promotion Strategy

Sales promotion refers to tools, other than advertising, used to stimulate short-term demand. This includes coupons, free samples, contests, premiums, point-of-purchase material, etc. Customer, trade, and sales force promotions can be included in this section along with budgets and calendars (similar to the examples mentioned above).

**Figure 5.4 Media Calendar**

| Media | Jan | Feb | Mar | Apr | May | Jun | Jul | Aug | Sep | Oct | Nov | Dec | Summary |
|---|---|---|---|---|---|---|---|---|---|---|---|---|---|
| Direct mail | | | | | | | | | | | | | |
| First wave | | | | | | | | | | | | | |
| Second wave | | | | | | | | | | | | | |
| Third wave | | | | | | | | | | | | | |
| | | | | | | | | | | | | | |
| Magazine advertising | | | | | | | | | | | | | |
| Magazine A | | | | | | | | | | | | | |
| Magazine B | | | | | | | | | | | | | |
| Magazine C | | | | | | | | | | | | | |
| | | | | | | | | | | | | | |
| Newspaper | | | | | | | | | | | | | |
| Newspaper A | | | | | | | | | | | | | |
| Newspaper B | | | | | | | | | | | | | |
| Newspaper C | | | | | | | | | | | | | |
| | | | | | | | | | | | | | |
| Television | | | | | | | | | | | | | |
| | | | | | | | | | | | | | |
| Radio | | | | | | | | | | | | | |
| | | | | | | | | | | | | | |
| Other media | | | | | | | | | | | | | |

Sales support materials can be covered in this section or in the field sales section. Also, any trade show strategies, merchandising, or publicity that the company is involved in should be addressed.

### Field Sales Plan

The field sales plan is usually beyond a product manager's control, but there might be activities for which product managers are responsible or activities that must be performed to attain product goals. In those cases, they should be included in this portion of the annual marketing plan.

### Distribution Strategy

The distribution strategy section should contain a statement on general policies and the desired penetration or coverage. If there are any planned changes, such as adding/deleting intermediaries or creating programs to improve relationships, they should be mentioned here along with the "fit" into the positioning and overall marketing objectives.

### Product Support

The product support section should provide a general statement on the policies for warranty/guarantee and repair service as well as any anticipated changes. As always, this should be coordinated with the rest of the marketing program so that the positioning and marketing objectives are achieved.

## Reference

1. Betsy D. Gelb, "Why Rich Brands Get Richer, and What to Do about It," *Business Horizons* 35 (September-October 1992): 46.

## Checklist: Hints on Writing the Annual Product Marketing Plan

✓ Word your annual product marketing objectives so that they indicate what you want to accomplish during the next fiscal year to take advantage of identified opportunities and to overcome potential problems.

✓ Be sure the objectives are consistent with the long-term vision of the product line and company.

✓ Identify the group(s) of customers you are going to focus your energies and resources on during the next fiscal year. This becomes your target market(s).

✓ Since many competitors could be going after this same group of customers, use your positioning statement to explain how you want customers to view you as better than the competition and how you can provide evidence of this difference.

✓ Consider the impact that pricing, advertising, field selling, distribution strategy and product support have on each other as well as on the success of your product. Write the marketing plan with these impacts in mind.

# Case Two

## The Importance of Data

Marketing plans can be effective only if based on a realistic analysis of data. Otherwise they are simply budgets with subjective inputs. Product managers collect and maintain data for the marketing plan in a product fact book, a compendium providing the nuts and bolts of the planning process. This case describes the product fact book Colgate-Palmolive uses in its product rollouts, then summarizes the key points in the marketing planning process for Chrysler's Neon.

### Colgate-Palmolive's Bundle Book

Colgate-Palmolive has adapted the idea of a product fact book into what it calls a bundle book—a three-ring binder containing everything the company knows about a product or category—and uses it to create global brands. The bundle book is distributed to Colgate subsidiaries to provide consistency and uniformity in rolling out brands to different regions.

According to Sharen Kindel in "Selling by the Book" (*Sales & Marketing Management*), Colgate's bundle books provide descriptive plans for a product roll-out.

> Bundle books contain such information as: a product overview, a definition of the marketing opportunity, the product's uniqueness, a vision statement, the product family, a digest of consumer research, packaging, graphics, and pricing strategy. Also included are the advertising plan, support materials, a professional relations program, information pertaining to advertising

claim substantiation, and even specific advertising executions. The book will answer questions regarding such technical issues as the formula, additives, fragrance, color and stability and provide a list of key contacts to check information or answer questions. Says John Steele [head of global business development], "We send the subsidiaries the kind of advertising we want. They're tested ads that are already working in some markets." Detailed country profiles provide specifics on the rollout plan and how the brand has performed to date. Information on competitive brands and their advertising support is also included.

The bundle books can be 150 to 200 pages in length and in some situations can exceed one volume. When Colgate launched its Colgate Total toothpaste in 1993, the launch was preceded by 18 months of research, resulting in a two-volume book. One volume contained the results of test marketing in six countries, carefully selected to provide a representative range of countries facing different marketing opportunities and constraints. The second volume covered public relations and advertising claim substantiation. Advertising, packaging, pricing, and positioning were consistent among all subsidiaries. Using the bundle book, Colgate's subsidiaries were able to launch Total in 66 countries within two years, the fastest global launch in Colgate's history.

The material in Colgate's bundle book provides the essence of the background analysis for product marketing planning as well as details about the action program. Although Colgate emphasizes its use for global new product rollouts, the basic concepts are appropriate for annual planning as well.

The *business assessment* coincides with the general culture of the company and its impact on the plan. In Colgate's case, the books were in line with the centralized marketing philosophy of the company.

Colgate prefers to give direction to its subsidiaries, whereas one of its major competitors, Unilever, allows its subsidiaries more freedom in the use of specific marketing tactics.

The *market analysis* focuses on selecting the appropriate customers for allocation of resources. For Colgate, the bundle books provide a consistent way of looking at the market—even small, fragmented markets. They provide input on the demographic and psychographic profiles of consumers most likely to use the products. This helps subsidiaries uncover new segments that are highly profitable or are underserved by the competition.

The *competitive strategy* depends on Colgate's relative position within a category. Since toothpaste is a core product for Colgate, the launch of Total required global speed to preempt competitors from bringing out a competing product and limiting its effectiveness. In the bleach category, a different approach was necessary. Colgate had just recently entered this business through acquisitions. Therefore the competitive portion of the bundle book contained new information to educate employees. The competitive portion should identify the competitors' general strategies, product differentiation, future moves, and consumer perceptions.

The *performance history,* since Colgate's bundle books focus on new products, contains test market results. Colgate tested Total in Australia, Columbia, Greece, the Philippines, Portugal, and the United Kingdom. The information gathered on sampling, the use of television, and other variables were incorporated into the bundle book. For these books to be used for annual marketing planning, it would be necessary to compare planned versus actual sales figures, along with the related analysis of why they occurred.

*Trends* also played a role in Colgate's strategy. In the past, when there were few global brands and limited international technology, there was little need for a standardized approach to megabrands. Now with the trend toward instantaneous communication (fax, electronic mail, or overnight courier can transmit information virtually anywhere in the world) the value of the bundle book in providing a common brand strategy makes sense.

### Key Points in Marketing Planning for the Chrysler Neon

Chrysler also went through significant analysis prior to developing the marketing plan for the Neon, its new subcompact car. A brief summary of the key points is presented here, using the format from the chapters in this section.

#### Background Analysis

The *business assessment*—the evaluation of Chrysler as a company—is the first part of the background analysis. Chrysler had both positive and negative points relative to marketing a subcompact car. First, it demonstrated stronger progress in improving its product development process than was true for the other American companies. This increased the likelihood of controlling development costs, thereby producing an affordable car. Second, it was committed to bringing out a successful small car and had, in fact, considered a joint deal with Fiat.

On the negative side, Chrysler had the worst quality record of the Big Three. Its prior attempts to enter the small-car market were dismal. In 1992 the Dodge Shadow and Plymouth Sundance had 162 problems and 137 problems, respectively, per 100 cars, according to J.D. Power. The only car with a worse record was the Hyundai Excel.

The *market analysis* was favorable. Both the domestic and foreign markets represented growing potential for subcompacts. Marketing research among current subcompact owners showed they wanted a small car that felt like a big one yet was fun to drive, safe, and reliable. Young families viewed this type of car as a utility vehicle. In terms of features, customers indicated a willingness to forego power windows and a four-speed automatic transmission in exchange for a reasonable price (base price approximately $9,000). Nevertheless, safety was paramount.

There were several *competitors* on the market, but they were generally higher-cost producers. Ford's new Escort, developed with Mazda, took five years to develop at a cost of $2 billion. When it was introduced, it turned out to be a rough-riding car, causing Ford to start selling it at $9,995 (a $500 loss per car according to analysts). Saturn was a formidable competitor, but with 7 years of development, the cost was estimated at $5 billion. Japanese subcompacts still had a high-quality image, but the average costs in 1993 were 13 percent more than in 1991, with a related market share drop from 52% to 49%. The competitive comparison as presented in *Business Week* in early 1993 is in the table in this case.

Since the Neon had not yet been introduced there were no sales, quality, or other *performance measures* to track. However, pre-launch checks were extensive. Test drivers logged unprecedented hours, with several early prototypes achieving 250,000 miles.

*Trends* were also favorable for the Neon. Federal mileage standards were expected to rise, forcing the automotive companies to increase

## Neon's Competitive Features

| | Price | Base engine/ horsepower | Weight in pounds | Fuel mpg | Driver air bags | Passenger air bags |
|---|---|---|---|---|---|---|
| Neon | $8,600-$12,500 | 2-liter/130 | 2,300 | 30+ (est) | standard | standard |
| Honda Civic | $8,950-$16,080 | 1.5-liter/102 | 2,300 | 38 | standard | optional |
| Ford Escort | $8,335-$11,923 | 1.9-liter/88 | 2,300 | 33 | N/A | N/A |
| GM Saturn | $9,395-$13,570 | 1.9 liter/85 | 2,300 | 36 | standard | N/A |
| Nissan Sentra | $8,995-$15,020 | 1.6 liter/110 | 2,400 | 35 | optional | N/A |
| Toyota Tercel | $7,998-$12,038 | 1.5 liter/82 | 2,000 | 29 | standard | N/A |

their development of cars with good gas mileage. Also, the recession spurred more interest in smaller, affordable cars.

### Synthesis

An examination of the background analysis yields several problems and opportunities. A primary challenge to overcome is the American market's perception that Chrysler products had low quality. This would need to be attacked by incorporating extra quality features into the car and using marketing communications effectively to combat the image. Chrysler also realized that they could attain their target price and still be profitable only if sales approached their capacity of 300,000 cars per year. This figure was well above any competing sub-compact sales figures, but the company had to shoot for this goal to make the project successful at the target price.

Based on that information, the Neon marketing objectives were to sell 300,000 cars, of which 10 percent would be at base price. The domestic models would be available January 1994, with European models rolling out four months later in April. The positioning approach would be reminiscent of the Volkswagen beetle positioning in the early 1960s. The Neon would be positioned as "youthful, lively and a little bit huggable," a functional car at a good price.

### Action Program

The primary target market was "Generation X" individuals in the 18-32 year-old range, earning in the mid-$20,000s; college students were part of this segment. Boomers over 35 with income in the low $40,000s were a secondary market. These groups were somewhat cynical and hard to sell, but consistent with the positioning of functional value.

The product, the Neon itself, was designed to appeal to the described target market, to attack the quality perception, and to achieve the target price. The Neon has a long wheelbase (seven inches longer than the Toyota Corolla) to allow more room in the rear seat. The cab-forward look allowed a high roof to be carried over the passenger compartment to provide more front and back headroom. These features provided the big-car "feel" the marketing research indicated was important to future customers. To attack the issue of safety, Neon became the first subcompact with standard dual air bags. It also incorporated reinforced doors to meet the 1997 federal side-impact standard, anti-lock brakes on all models, and height-adjustable front belts. In terms of achieving the target price, the base Neon was designed with crank windows and similar spartan features, consistent with input from consumers.

The base price was approximately $9,457, ringing in at $850 less than the cheapest four-door Saturn. However, several option packages allow a "nicely-loaded" Neon to be available for $11,000 to $13,000. A popularly-equipped version will cost about $12,000 with a Sport model carrying a $13,000 price tag.

Early promotional strategies relied heavily on advance publicity. News articles in business and consumer publications, test drive reports from automotive journalists and industry analysts, and various feature stories provided credible support for Chrysler's product development process and renewed control over quality. An estimated $80 million was budgeted for the marketing campaign. BBDO, the advertising agency for the product, broke the debut campaign on the SuperBowl. A blizzard of billboard ads near dealers pictured the front of the car with the simple headline, "Hi," to bring to life the desired positioning of "youthful, lively and a little bit huggable." Television, radio and print advertising were consistent with and reinforced the message on the billboards. Care was taken to avoid pigeon-holing the younger generation. Instead of using MTV-style advertising or stereotyping

Generation X, the campaign focused on communicating product benefits while developing a huggable personality for the car.

The distribution strategy was to sell the Neon under the same brand name to both Dodge and Plymouth dealers. This tactic was intended to reinforce to the cynical target market that Chrysler wasn't using superficial differentiation to sell the car through the two separate dealer networks. By creating a single model name, Neon, in effect, became the brand. This approach enabled the company to get more benefit from its advertising investment.

Source: Adapted from Sharen Kindel, "Selling by the Book," *Sales & Marketing Management,* October 1994, 101-107; David Woodruff and Karen Lowry Miller, "Chrysler's Neon," *Business Week,* May 3, 1993, 116-126; Patrick Bedard, "Dodge Neon," *Car and Driver,* April 1994, 55-59; Neon promotional literature.

# SECTION THREE

# PRODUCT SKILLS

Most product managers have responsibility for both existing and new products. For existing products, the product manager is expected to (1) maintain a database or fact book; (2) evaluate product performance; (3) add value; (4) increase market penetration; and (5) evaluate the product line.

The ongoing product analysis, along with external input on the customers and competition, will trigger ideas for line extensions and totally new concepts. The process of turning these ideas into commercially viable products is often a company endeavor, coordinated by the product manager. He or she can play a vital role in idea generation, screening, concept development and testing, prototype testing, pre-launch, launch, and project evaluation.

This section addresses the analytical skills a product manager needs to evaluate an existing product line, as well as to determine and implement new-product strategies.

# 6

# EVALUATING THE
# PRODUCT PORTFOLIO

Much of a product manager's time will be spent evaluating and
improving on existing products and on modifications of the product
line. Even if the product is the same for a while, the marketing strategy might need to change. A routine examination of the product line
should uncover the types of changes necessary for optimizing the company's product position. If a product manager is responsible for a limited number of products, it might be possible to conduct thorough
analyses of each. However, the reality for most companies is that the
Pareto rule applies: 80 percent of the sales and/or profits come from
20 percent of the products. These most important products should
have constant attention, with the rest receiving periodic attention.

There are five activities the product manager should perform relative to evaluating the product portfolio. First, the product manager
must maintain (or establish) a database of relevant information on the

product. Second, the products must be evaluated in terms of customer satisfaction, competition, and company expectations. Third, the product manager must add value to existing products by improving features, adding an element of competitive superiority, and/or reducing costs. Fourth, the product manager should attempt to increase market penetration by appealing to more users or increasing the usage rate of existing customers. And, finally, the product manager must evaluate the product line to look for gaps where new products need to be developed and/or to determine when to delete products.

## Maintain a Database on Existing Products

The product manager's first job related to evaluating the product portfolio is to ensure that product-related information is in a form conducive to analysis and decision making. This is the product fact book, where all relevant information is in a central location. The information in the fact book can be held in a three-ring binder, a manual filing system, or an electronic database.

There is no one right way to set up a database; it depends on the needs of the product manager. Typically there will be files on customer profiles and changes; the perceived importance of various product features; the major competitors and their strengths and weaknesses; the sales/profit/contribution history of the product or product line; and technological or macroeconomic trends that could impact product sales in the future.

The information in the database must be updated periodically through marketing research, input from the customer service department, sales force input, on-line database searching, and/or published information from trade publications.

## Evaluate Product Performance

The beginning point for a product performance evaluation is the audit performed as part of the performance history portion of the background analysis (see Chapter 4). This should have triggered problems and opportunities related to features, potential new-product entries, and/or quality issues that should be addressed in the product plan for the upcoming fiscal year. Aspects to evaluate about product performance include sales/profits by customer segment, channel of distribution, or geographic region; the complementary value of the product to others in the line; seasonal fluctuations in demand; the awareness and preference level for the product; rate of repeat purchases (retention); and the planned to actual performance.

Product managers should avoid thinking about existing products as mature, but should rather treat them as "core brands." Think about the brands as if they were being acquired from another company; envision the possibilities. Study customers to find out not only their buyer behavior, but also what causes that behavior.[1]

Product managers frequently use competitive matrices to study their products. A competitive matrix is a visual display of one product versus the competition along two axes. Each axis is a continuum of an attribute such as ease of use, comfort, price, etc. The selection of attributes should be based on what is important to customers.

A competitive matrix (sometimes called a perceptual map) focuses attention on the relative competitive positioning a product has along significant factors. (See Figure 6.1.) Start by determining what is most important to a customer in making a buying decision. Ask customers to list and rank attributes in terms of priority and to assess how significant those attributes truly are in terms of affecting their purchase decisions.

## Figure 6.1  Competitive Matrix (Perceptual Map)

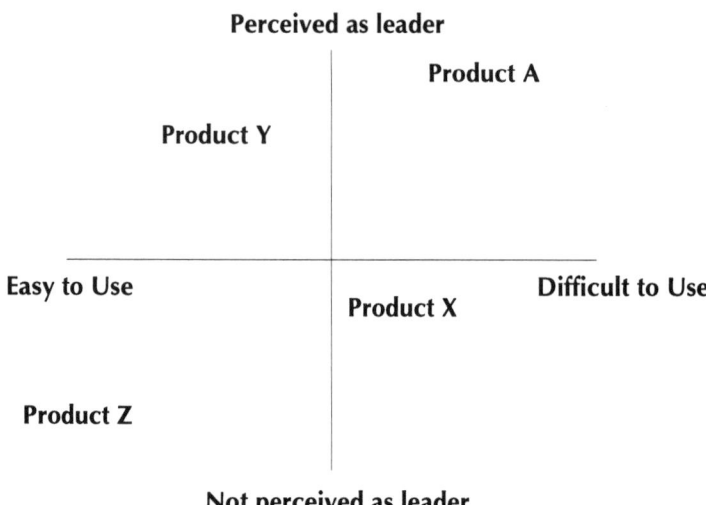

Then select the top two or four attributes to utilize for the relative positioning of significant competitors along each attribute. For example, assume that Product A is compared with competing products X, Y, and Z along two important purchase criteria: leadership in the market and ease of use. Note that A is perceived as a leader to a greater degree than the competition; this could be used as part of its positioning strategy. However, it is also perceived as more difficult to use than any of the competitors. This could suggest a strategy of providing clearer instructions and/or redesigning the product to make it easier to use.

Another approach to this, when several factors are deemed equally important, is to list all factors as continua and ask customers to rate each product along each factor. The average or mean responses for each competitive product can be joined by a line to indicate the "profile" of each. In Figure 6.2, three products are being evaluated against each other. Product A is perceived as slightly superior in terms of product consistency, Product B is easiest to use, and Product C has better delivery.

## Add Value to Existing Products

Both the competitive matrix and profile approaches just described compare a product against its competitors along established factors. The typical objective is to improve attributes that are competitively

## Figure 6.2  Comparative Product Scaling

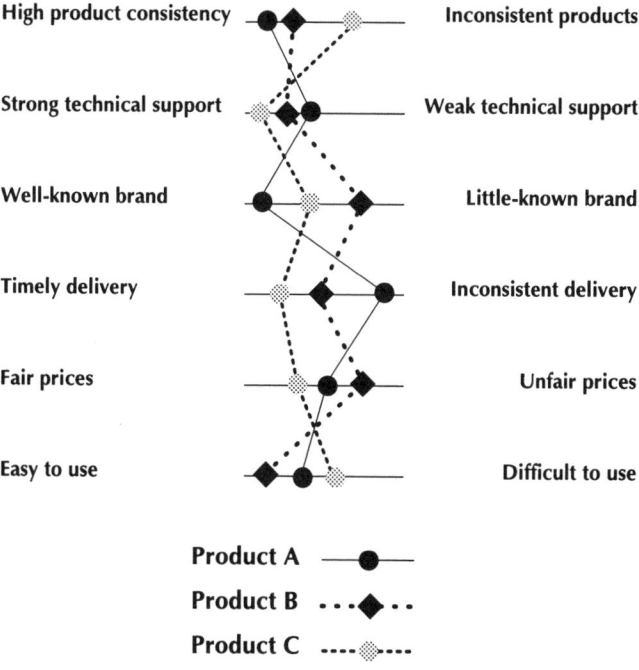

High product consistency     Inconsistent products

Strong technical support     Weak technical support

Well-known brand     Little-known brand

Timely delivery     Inconsistent delivery

Fair prices     Unfair prices

Easy to use     Difficult to use

Product A  —●—

Product B  ...◆..

Product C  ----◈---

weak. What is generally missing is the internal cost of the specific factors. Sometimes a product can be made more profitable by reducing the cost of unimportant attributes. If this also results in a price reduction, the result can be more value to the customer. Therefore, it is useful to add cost information to the perceived importance and competitive performance of each attribute, as shown in Figure 6.3.

Note that the first column starts with features and attributes of the product. These have to be converted to benefits in the second column. The average importance of each benefit to the market must be determined (through marketing research) or estimated (from informal customer input) and listed in the third column. The next column indicates how well the product supplies the benefit relative to the competition. The final column indicates whether the cost of the related features are a significant proportion of the overall cost of the product.

Look for red flags in the table. The provision of benefits that are highly important to the market should be from features that are at least equal to or better than the competition in terms of performance. If that is not the case, the product manager should improve on those features. If features provide benefits that are not important to the cus-

## Figure 6.3  Costs and Benefits of Features Relative to the Market

| Features/ Attributes | Benefits | Importance to Market | Competitive Performance | Relative Cost |
|---|---|---|---|---|
|  |  |  |  |  |

tomer, the relative cost should be low. Otherwise, the feature should be eliminated or provided at as low a cost as possible.

This type of analysis should precede quality improvement and cost reduction programs. By working with teams from other parts of the company, the product manager can use value analysis, quality function deployment, or other techniques to increase customer satisfaction without a commensurate increase in costs or maintain customer satisfaction while lowering costs.

It is important to continually rethink and redefine the product creatively to look for opportunities hidden behind the day-to-day grind. What would happen if some features were magnified? Minimized? What if a new product replaced this one? Can two existing products be combined to provide one with more value to the customer? Can certain elements be modified? Can the development process be reengineered to reduce the overall cost of producing the product or service? Can the traditional approach be changed—e.g., can direct mail be used as an alternative to the traditional method of distributing the product? (See Figure 6.4.)

After identifying features that deserve detailed examination, the next job of the product manager is to benchmark these features against the "best-in-class." Start by finding out from salespeople, customers, and industry writings what company or product is recognized as best for the aspect under study. Then strive to uncover why it is perceived as best. For example, when Ford redesigned the 1992 Taurus, it benchmarked more than 200 features against seven competitors. Door handles were benchmarked against the Chevy Lumina, headlamps against the Accord, and remote radio controls against the Pontiac Grand Prix.[2]

However, benchmarking should not be limited to the competition and it does not have to be limited to product features. By

## Figure 6.4  Rethinking Your Product

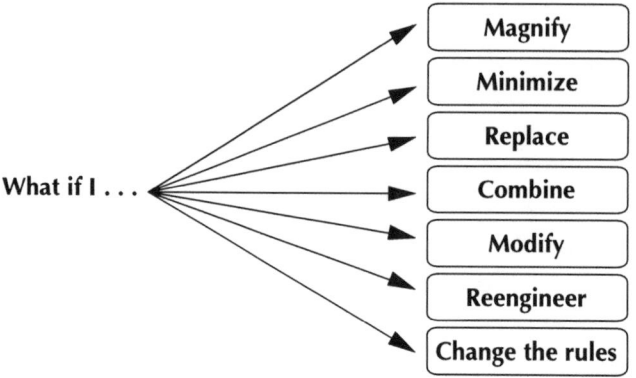

improving processes used to deliver a product or service, it is possible to provide more value for the customer. Mellon Bank in Pittsburgh, for example, undertook a benchmarking project to improve its credit card billing practices. By benchmarking seven other companies, including an airline, they learned about techniques and software technologies to improve the process. After adopting several improvements they cut outstanding complaints by half and were able to resolve problems in an average of 25 days instead of the 45 days it took previously.[3]

## Increase Market Penetration

Another tactic the product manager could use is to boost sales volume by increasing the number of users and/or the usage rate per user. The number of users can be increased by winning competitors' customers, entering new market segments, and/or converting nonusers into users. Volume can also be increased by finding new applications for the product or by encouraging more frequent usage.

To increase the number of users, a product manager must collect three types of information: (1) why competitors' customers buy from the competition; (2) what, if anything, could convince nonusers to become users of the product; and (3) what market segments are attractive and accessible. Information for the first two items on the list can be obtained partly through sales input in the way of lost order reports. However, this is at best an incomplete picture, because not all customers are contacted by the sales force. Therefore, if this is critical data, some additional research is necessary. Focus groups and one-on-one interviews can uncover new insights into why customers choose alternative products or choose none at all.

To identify what segments are attractive and accessible requires a combination of information and intuition. Start by profiling existing customer segments that have shown higher than average increases in sales. Determine whether these increases are unique to the product's customers or whether noncustomers with similar profiles have also exhibited a need for the product. Then assess whether the total segment (customers and noncustomers) is growing or declining in sheer size. Also look for segments that have suddenly appeared and have specific needs not being addressed by the competition.

## Evaluate the Product Line

In evaluating a product line, the product manager can use the same steps discussed in this chapter previously, particularly when the line is comprised of fast-moving consumer goods (FMCG). First, data need to be maintained on each item in the line. Second, relative product performance needs to be evaluated. This includes an examination of customer behavior for the entire line. Try to determine whether customers can substitute a filler product if the core product is out of stock or whether they are apt to buy a competing product. Third, increase value to the product line by (a) adding products that enhance the competitive positioning and increase brand equity; or (b) deleting products that are not important to the target market and simply increase costs. Finally, increase market penetration by generating more usage through a carefully planned marketing communications strategy.

Regularly evaluate the product line to look for gaps to be filled or products to be eliminated. Product managers frequently use portfolio matrices as visual tools to compare products within a line. A common matrix is the product-market attractiveness model developed by General Electric working with McKinsey & Co. (See Figure 6.5.) This matrix groups products into nine categories, along some combination of business strength and market attractiveness. Products are evaluated as low, medium, or high in terms of business strength and market

**Figure 6.5  Product/Market Attractiveness**

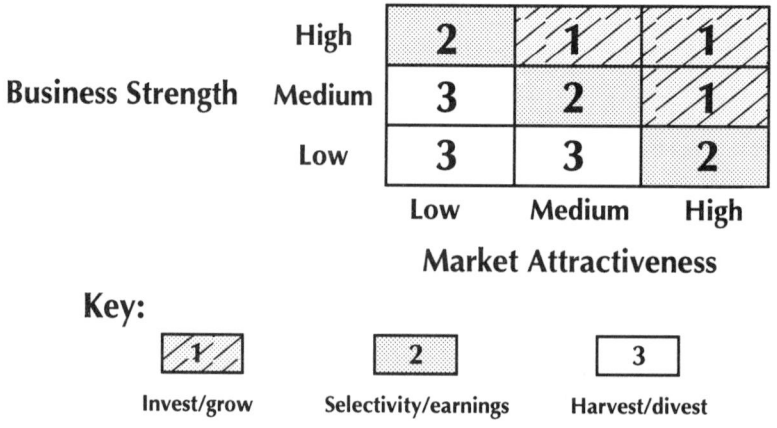

Source: General Electric/McKinsey & Co.

attractiveness. Business strength includes items such as whether the particular product is a core product of the company based on its competencies, the market share of the particular product, and the profitability of the product. Market attractiveness includes such factors as market growth rate, competitiveness within the product category, and strategic importance of the market to the company.

Products in the "1" cells have a strong position and should be enhanced through additional investment. Products in the "3" cells are weak and should be evaluated carefully to determine whether there is significant complementary value to retain them, or whether they should be dropped. If a product elimination is being considered, there must be a careful examination of overhead cost absorption. Sometimes a weak product is at least covering all direct costs and contributing to overhead. If it is dropped, it is possible that the overhead would be allocated to other products, possibly making them marginal as well. Products in the "2" cells are questionable, and money should be invested selectively in them.

This matrix is simply an example of one that any company could develop. Choose the variables of most importance in evaluating the line and determine the best way to categorize the existing products.

If a company does not have a product-review committee, recommend that one be established. The committee should be comprised of representatives from marketing, manufacturing, and finance. The committee should develop a company-appropriate system for identifying weak products. The system would specify how frequently to meet (e.g., quarterly, annually), what criteria to examine (number of years of sales decline, market changes, gross margin, etc.), and procedures for product elimination. Whatever recommendations are made should be included in the annual plan with rationale and a statement of the impact on the overall marketing program.

## References

1. James R. Tindall, "Marketing Established Brands," *Journal of Consumer Marketing,* 8 (Fall 1991): 5-10.

2. Jeremy Main, "How to Steal the Best Ideas Around," *Fortune,* October 19, 1992, 103.

3. Ibid.

---

## Checklist: Tips on Evaluating the Product Portfolio

---

✓ Before evaluating your products in depth, prioritize them in terms of their profitability and strategic potential. Practice the 80/20 rule.

✓ Collect and maintain information on your products, your customers, and your competition on an ongoing basis.

✓ Determine the features or attributes of your product (including supporting services) of highest importance to your customers, then regularly compare these against the best-in-class products and companies.

✓ Don't limit your analysis to what customers say is important now; challenge yourself to rethink and redefine the product to uncover hidden opportunities for the future.

✓ Remember that the markets for your products aren't static; look for new ways to increase users and usage.

✓ In addition to examining individual products, study the total product line or mix you offer your customers. Weed out weak products and add new products to fill in the gaps as appropriate.

# 7

# STRATEGIC PRODUCT PLANNING

Strategic product planning requires an understanding of corporate and divisional strategic goals. Most long-term visions have some implicit (or explicit) statement of the future "picture" of the company and its product offerings. The product manager has to understand the role his or her product(s) play in this vision. It is not enough to know the percentage of profits expected from a new product line, although that is important information. The product manager must also know what new markets, new technologies, and new directions should be incorporated into the long-term product plan.

Strategic product thinking is different from new-product development (discussed in the next chapter), because it forces product managers to envision a future that does not yet exist . . . to lead the market and create products before customers ask for them. This requires a certain level of risk and creativity. Product managers must ask themselves: How will the customers of tomorrow be different from the customers of today? What products/services will these customers expect? What existing capabilities can we expect to use in the future and what new abilities will we need to develop? The emphasis is not on projecting the present into the future. Rather, the emphasis is on trying to understand how the future will be different from the present and the impact that will have on present planning.

## Fostering a Customer Mind-Set

This requires the product manager to step back and redefine the business in terms of customer functions. It may also require redefining what it means to satisfy the customer. When David Whitwam became CEO of Whirlpool in 1987, his vision was to transform the company into a customer-focused organization and to shift thinking from product to customer, as indicated in the following excerpt from an interview with *Harvard Business Review:*

> The starting point isn't the existing product; it's the function consumers buy products to accomplish. When you return to first principles, the design issues dramatically change. The microwave couldn't have been invented by someone who assumed he or she was in the business of designing a range. Such a design breakthrough required seeing that the opportunity is "easier, quicker food preparation," not "a better range."
>
> Take the "fabric-care business," which we used to call the "washing-machine business." We're now studying consumer behavior from the time people take off their dirty clothes at night until they've been cleaned and ironed and hung in the closet. What are we looking for? The worst part of the process

is not the washing and drying. The hard part is when you take your clothes out of the dryer and you have to do something with them—iron, fold, hang them up. Whoever comes up with a product to make this part of the process easier, simpler, or quicker is going to create an incredible market.[1]

Before continuing this section on strategic product planning, complete the quiz on "Assessing Your Company's Strategic IQ", shown as Figure 7.1.

## Understanding Past Successes and Failures

Another step in strategic evaluation is to calculate a company's "hit rate" in new products and determine the reasons for it. Compare successful product launches with unsuccessful ones. What were the common elements of successful development efforts that were different from unsuccessful development efforts? Was there a difference in R&D investment and shared communication? The number of ideas generated? The sequence of steps in the development process? The understanding of the market? The application of core competencies? All of these can be significant factors and must be part of the strategic thinking process.

R&D and manufacturing personnel are important contributors to successful strategic product planning. Product managers should determine with manufacturing how wide a product line can be without putting a strain on efficiency. This includes understanding how future products can be developed from a common platform, as Hewlett-Packard has done with its ink-jet printers. Prevent product proliferation by deciding which products can be dropped when new

## Figure 7.1  Assessing Your Company's Strategic IQ

*Read each of the following questions and evaluate your firm on a 1-5 scale (for statements 1-10) or a 1-10 scale (for statements 11-15) with 1 = Poor and the top value (5 or 10) = Excellent.*

_____ 1. The company has a clear-cut vision of what it will look like in the future.

_____ 2. The strategic vision is stated concisely to avoid overloading the organization with competing (and possibly conflicting) initiatives.

_____ 3. Strategic thinking (broad-based, unrestricted) coexists with strategic planning (narrower and more detailed in focus).

_____ 4. The company emphasizes leveraging its resources to move toward an ambitious vision rather than restricting its vision to fit current resources.

_____ 5. In making outsourcing, divestiture, and product elimination decisions, the impact of the decision on core capabilities is considered.

_____ 6. In making acquisition decisions, the impact on core capabilities is considered.

_____ 7. There is a competitive focus throughout the organization and a widespread use of competitive intelligence.

_____ 8. The company uses competitive innovation at least as frequently as (if not more frequently than) competitive imitation.

_____ 9. Key members in all departments throughout the company are aware of market trends that could impact the strategy.

_____10. The strategic plan plays an integral role in the development of annual marketing plans.

*Note: The next five statements are worth 10 points each.*

_____ 11. The company has studied its historical track record to

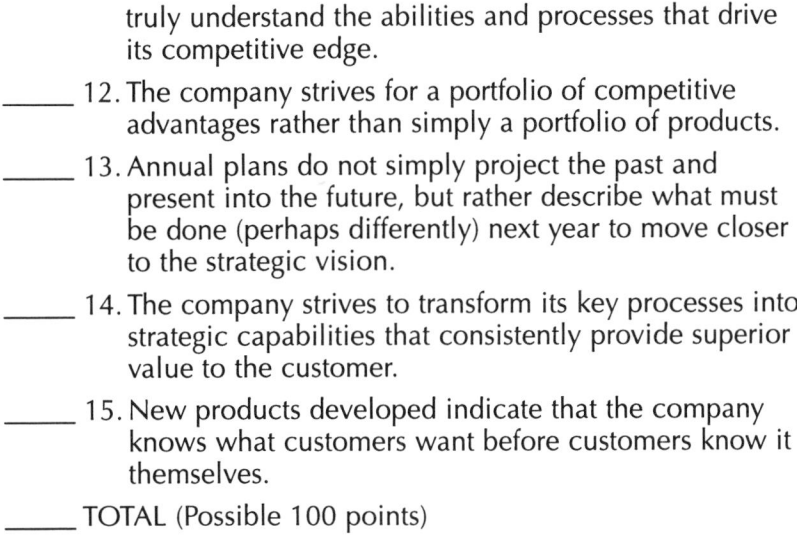

truly understand the abilities and processes that drive its competitive edge.

_____ 12. The company strives for a portfolio of competitive advantages rather than simply a portfolio of products.

_____ 13. Annual plans do not simply project the past and present into the future, but rather describe what must be done (perhaps differently) next year to move closer to the strategic vision.

_____ 14. The company strives to transform its key processes into strategic capabilities that consistently provide superior value to the customer.

_____ 15. New products developed indicate that the company knows what customers want before customers know it themselves.

_____ TOTAL (Possible 100 points)

ones are introduced. If products are not to be dropped, the product manager must lobby for increased R&D and/or operations support to attain the strategic product goals.

## Developing Product Ideas

The number of ideas generated can affect successful product commercialization by increasing the likelihood of uncovering the best product concepts. Although many argue that there is no shortage of ideas per se, it can also be argued that many good ideas never surface because the available ideas are "good enough." Product managers are frequently under pressure to generate new products quickly. Because they also juggle existing products at the same time, they do not allow themselves the luxury of thoroughly examining all alternatives. They resort to line extensions or "me-too" products because thinking is muddied by the present. That is why strategic gestation of ideas can be a useful prelude to product development.

There are several sources of strategic product ideas. An important source is customers and potential customers. Unfortunately, too many companies don't use a disciplined approach to obtain futuristic ideas. For business-to-business products, a useful research approach is a systematic customer visit program. A customer visit program is a structured approach to data collection through which specific customers are targeted for their expected contributions to an issue being studied, company personnel are recruited to participate in the program due to their importance to the decision being made, and written objectives are established for the data collection. Customers who are future-thinkers, who are industry leaders, or who have unique applications for the product are asked to participate in the program. A small group of people from R&D, operations, and marketing are briefed on the goal of the project, and arrangements are made to call on the selected customers. The resulting insights from the customer visit program are then synthesized into potential long-term product ideas. Trade shows are another vehicle for reaching customers. Conducting a focus group at a trade show can be a lower-cost alternative for obtaining new product ideas.

Brainstorming sessions focused on a particular goal can also be a valuable tool for product development. During the session, participants are encouraged to think in terms of metaphors and analogies. The application of analogies was used successfully when Canon was attempting to develop a disposable drum for its mini-copiers.

> Canon designers knew that for the first personal copier to be successful, it had to be reliable. To ensure reliability, they proposed to make the product's photosensitive copier drum—

which is the source of 90% of all maintenance problems—disposable. To be disposable, however, the drum would have to be easy and cheap to make. How to manufacture a throwaway drum?

The breakthrough came one day when task-force leader Hiroshi Tanaka ordered out for some beer. As the team discussed design problems over their drinks, Tanaka held one of the beer cans and wondered aloud, "How much does it cost to manufacture this can?" The question led the team to speculate whether the same process for making an aluminum beer can could be applied to the manufacture of an aluminum copier drum. By exploring how the drum actually is and is not like a beer can, the mini-copier development team was able to come up with the process technology that could manufacture an aluminum drum at the appropriate low cost.[2]

Product managers must also be aware of the company's core competencies and be willing to work with other functional areas and other product managers to leverage these skills into future products and markets. (see "Strategic Leveraging at 3M and Hewlett-Packard). Rubbermaid, for example, encourages its employees to focus on the abilities of other parts of the company and use them if possible in their areas.

Rubbermaid teaches its people to let ideas flow out of its so-called core competencies, the things it does best. Bud Hellman, who used to run a Rubbermaid subsidiary, was touring one of the company's picnic-cooler plants in the late Eighties when he suddenly realized he could use its plastic blow-molding techniques to make a durable, lightweight, and inexpensive line of office furniture. The result was the

―――――――――――― ▬▬▬▬▬▬ ――――――――――――

# Strategic Leveraging at 3M and Hewlett-Packard

Both 3M and Hewlett-Packard are recognized leaders in innovation and strategic product planning. Their success is due to several factors. An important one is the ability to leverage skills across divisions and into new market applications. Another is cannibalizing products before someone else does.

Going beyond cross-functional to cross-divisional thinking, 3M's CEO, L.D. DeSimone, is urging his R&D teams to apply proprietary technology wherever it can work. For example, focus group input suggested that consumers did not like the fact that steel wool soap pads rusted and frayed. Staff from both the tape and abrasives divisions worked together to create the Never Rust Wool Soap Pad, using fibers from recycled plastic bottles and an environmentally safe soap. Since its introduction in late 1992 it has become a close second in market share of the scouring-pad market, not far behind Clorox Company's S.O.S. pad, the market leader.

In another example of leveraging, 3M started marketing a film for laptop computer screens based on the film it first developed in the mid-1980s for decorative signs on buildings. This thin plastic film built into screens improves brightness and conserves energy, thereby extending the battery life of laptops.

Like 3M, Hewlett-Packard has been effective at strategic leveraging of its core capabilities. It recently combined its expertise in computers with its knowledge of patient- monitoring systems to create a physician's workstation. Although still in the field testing stage, it could greatly enlarge H-P's medical equipment business.

Hewlett-Packard also strives to use its key abilities in new and different ways. Since plain-paper fax machines use many of the same mechanisms as ink-jet printers, H-P has targeted this as one of its top candidates for product market growth. By using existing technology H-P expects to be able to develop these faxes at no more cost than those using thermal paper.

The ink-jet printers are also competing against H-P's well-known laser printers. According to CEO Lewis Platt this proactive self-destruction is necessary: "We have to be willing to cannibalize what we're doing today in order to ensure our leadership in the future. It's counter to human nature, but you have to kill your business while it is still working."

Source: Adapted from Kevin Kelly, "The Drought is over at 3M," *Business Week* November 7, 1994, 140-141; and Alan Deutschman, "How H-P Continues to Grow and Grow," *Fortune* May 2, 1994, 90-100.

---

WorkManager System, which the company says accounts for 60% of its furniture division sales. Says Charles Hassel, a member of the product development team: "If top management hadn't encouraged us to look at processes and technologies elsewhere in the company, none of this would have ever happened."[3]

# Targeting Current, Tangential, and New Markets

Products can have varying levels of risk, and it is usually wise to have a portfolio of new products to balance the risk/return equation. New products with the lowest risk are line extensions—slight modifications (New and improved! versions) of an existing product. Larger or smaller package sizes, stronger or weaker flavors, and lighter or heavier components are all examples of line extensions. Most of these modifications are intended to increase usage among or provide more options for current customers. Sometimes the same (or a slightly different) product can be repositioned to attain usage among tangential markets. The classic example of this is baking soda, which was repositioned for numerous applications beyond baking. Bayer pain reliever extended to five models to increase usage among tangential markets such as people with arthritis. Finally, taking the existing product to a new market can be potentially profitable, but it must be marketed correctly. For example, the Bendix Brake Division of Allied Signal wanted to increase its brake sales in the do-it-yourself (DIY) market. It discovered that its packaging didn't connote high quality, so it redesigned its packaging to incorporate a strong color blue as part of the repositioning strategy. In one year its sales moved from less than 1 percent market share to more than 20 percent.

Products that are more than line extensions are also new and can be marketed to the same customer segments, tangential segments, or totally new markets. Of these three alternatives, the least risky is reaching the existing customer base through franchise extensions. A franchise extension (also referred to as a brand extension) refers to taking what the product (or brand) connotes and applying it in a different product category. For example, Arm & Hammer baking soda

---

## The Power of Line Extensions

Extending a franchise offers a number of benefits which traditional new-product development does not. The major one is that extension capitalizes on the company's most valuable assets—its brand names. Thus, the company moves into a new category from a position of strength. . . . A further benefit is that investment outlays typically necessary to establish a new brand—a significant expense—are minimal.

A consumer is exposed to hundreds of brand names every day. Being a well-known brand is not sufficient to be a good brand extension. Few consumers want JELL-O shoelaces or Tide frozen entrees. A brand can be successfully extended to a new category when it has both *fit* and *leverage.*

- *Fit* is when the consumer accepts the new product as logical and would expect it from the brand.
- *Leverage* is when the consumer, by simply knowing the brand, can think of important ways that they perceive the new brand extension would be better than competing products in the category.

Since a brand's meaning can change over time as brand extensions are introduced, management needs to develop a *brand plan*—what extensions are introduced short term and what others become possible long term. Note the changing possibilities Ocean Spray faced as they moved from cranberries to cranberry juice, to being a full-line bottled juice supplier. One must develop a long-term scenario to avoid diluting important elements of the brand and to improve the odds of pursuing more remote areas where the brand could have leverage.

Source: Edward M. Tauber, "Brand Leverage: Strategy for Growth in a Cost-Control World," *Journal of Advertising Research* (August/September 1988): 28.

---

extended its brand franchise to detergent, toothpaste, and similar products for which the concept of "clean and fresh" was appropriate. Castle & Cooke found that its Dole brand connoted more than pineapple and used the brand name to launch Dole Fruit & Juice bars. These types of extensions can have definite benefits, but they require some strategic thinking and planning.

Flanker brands are used when a company wants to enter a slightly different market segment (e.g., the "cost-conscious segment") but does not want to dilute its current image. Flanker brands allow a company to retain its current position with existing customers, while still expanding into different segments. Marriott has used flanker brands to extend its position. Fairfield Inn is a low-price, low-frills product of the Marriott chain. Oldsmobile was forced to rethink the value of its brand identity when it introduced the Aurora. After a significant corporate debate, Olds decided to take its "rocket" logo (a traditional Oldsmobile symbol) off the car—at least for now—and replace it with a silver script A to attract younger buyers.[4]

The riskiest approach is to create a new product for a new market, especially if the product is not just new to the company but also new to the world. Unless the new market can be reached through existing distribution channels and/or the product can build on core competencies, this is a questionable endeavor. The company must carefully assess whether the risk is worth the effort, whether it will be possible to develop and protect a competitive edge in the future, and even whether the idea is best left for the competition.

## References

1. Regina Fazio Maruca, "The Right Way to Go Global," *Harvard Business Review* 72 (March/April 1994): 143.

2. "The Knowledge-Creating Company," *Harvard Business Review* 69 (November/December 1991): 101.

3. Brian Dumaine, "Closing the Innovation Gap," *Fortune,* December 2, 1991, 59.

4. Kathleen Kerwin, "GM's Aurora," *Business Week,* March 21, 1994, 88-95.

## Checklist:  Preparing for Strategic Product Planning

✓ Challenge yourself to (at least occasionally) lead the market and create products before customers ask for them.

✓ Strive to build a portfolio of core capabilities rather than simply a portfolio of products.

✓ Understand the reasons for your past successes and failures in new product development.

✓ Work with engineers to understand and possibly implement a platform strategy for strategic product planning.

✓ Don't underestimate the need to come up with new product ideas. It's risky to assume that the new-product ideas you now have are the best you can come up with.

✓ Talk to other product managers, other divisions, and other units in your company to assess whether there are some capabilities you can leverage within your product area.

✓ If brands are crucial in your industry, create a vision for the future growth and development of the brand identity or brand equity.

# 8

# NEW PRODUCTS: PROPOSAL, DEVELOPMENT, AND LAUNCH

Companies have increasingly found that to be successful in new-product development, it is not enough to find out what customers want and create products for those wants. They must also be able to do it better than the competition by exploiting their core abilities. In addition, there must be clarity about the company's internal process of new-product development. The Medical Products Group of Hewlett-Packard, for example, uncovered 14 critical internal processes that differentiated successful and unsuccessful products.

> When executives at Hewlett-Packard's Medical Products Group studied 10 of their new-product failures along with 10 of their successes, they were surprised to identify a total of 14 essential tasks that determined which products

---

## Polaroid: Changes in New Product Development

Polaroid, with 1993 sales of $2.2 billion, has been floundering in the new product development front. Largely a niche player in the photography marketplace, the company's over-focus on its core abilities to the exclusion of related abilities (such as microprocessor technology) has left it unable to match the innovations that created Polaroid.

To begin attacking the problem, the company put together a benchmarking team to study how other companies handled product development. Their key recommendations were very similar to those endorsed by experts in the field. First, the company must adopt a good *process* of product development that works for the company. As Michael Hammer says in *Reengineering the Corporation: A Manifesto for Business Revolution,* "It is not products but the processes that create products that bring companies long-term success. Good products don't make winners; winners make good products." On a related note there has to be a strategy that encompasses both the current product line and potential new entrants. Next, focus should be placed on platforms rather than individual products. This is especially critical in the high-technology fields. Finally, core abilities should be leveraged when expanding into new markets.

Polaroid's Helios 810 Laser Imaging System, a new medical imager using a chemical-free digital process, was one of the first projects to benefit from the new-product regimen. The company established a cross-functional team early in the process to both share internal ideas and obtain customer input up-front. On the basis of the input, Polaroid decided to create a product that would produce pictures that could be used with the ultrasound and which would be in a format familiar to radiologists. The price point, throughput, speed, and other parameters were identified and frozen as early as possible. Beta testing was conducted in the form of a year of clinical trials in hospitals.

Tackling the launch was another problem. While the product leverages the company's dry-processing technology, it is moving into a new and unfamiliar market. "These are very much relationship-selling, long-sales-cycle products. It's very different from traditional Polaroid products so there was a lot of learning and effort into how we should bring this to a customer," says Roy Miller, director of new business development for Polaroid's High Resolution Imaging Organization. Consequently the launch documentation and process required significant care and cross-functional cooperation.

Although it's too soon to tell whether the Helios 810 Laser Imaging System will be a commercial success for Polaroid, they've still benefited from a defined new-product development process, and increased emphasis on customer contact, and the establishment of a system that will be useful for future endeavors at Polaroid.

Source: Adapted from Sharen Kindel, "Grape Expectations," *Sales & Marketing Management* (January 1995), 89-93.

worked and which didn't. The steps covered a wide range of corporate skills. Among them: figuring out which new products play to a company's core strengths, understanding how a new product should be sold, and getting an early fix on a project's costs.[1]

Product development involves many parts of a company, not just the product manager. But because product managers are frequently charged with the ultimate success of a new product, it is important to discuss their involvement in the process. Although new-product development goes beyond the fiscal year planning horizon of the marketing plan for a product line, certain portions will need to be addressed each year. For some years, researching and submitting product proposals will be the extent of new-product efforts. At other times during the midst of the development project, milestones should be written into the annual plan. And, finally, as commercialization draws near, launch documentation will need to be developed and integrated into the annual plan.

Product innovation and speed of development are becoming increasingly important in our global economy. Although the role of the product manager in new-product development will vary by company, the product manager at minimum should take care in understanding and articulating the market potential and in participating on the product development team. We will examine the steps in the development process, along with the potential role of the product manager. (See Figures 8.1 and 8.2.)

Note that the first step of the new-product development process is idea generation. Ideas are fleshed out into a proposal and presented to top management (or a new-product review committee comprised of key executives of all the functional areas) for screening. For

## Figure 8.1 New Product Development Flow Chart

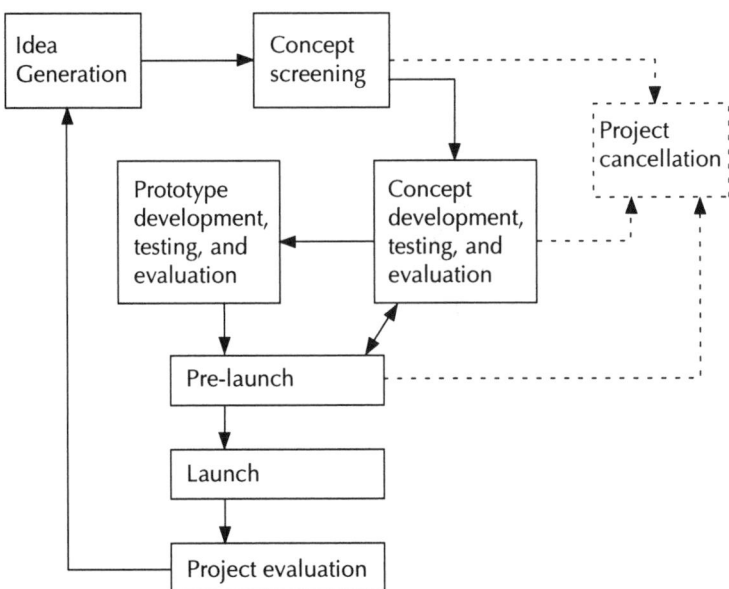

major product ideas/concepts that pass screening, management assigns representatives from relevant functional areas to a multifunctional project team for this particular new-product endeavor. The team members select a leader (who might or might not be the product manager) to organize and monitor the project, guiding it through the critical path schedule developed by the team. All members do as many tasks as possible in parallel to shorten the product development cycle. For example, product managers can conduct focus groups on concept evaluation at the same time that engineering is conducting technical feasibility studies. The dotted line from the concept development and evaluation box to the project cancellation box indicates that concepts testing poorly should be consid-

## Figure 8.2  Stages in New Product Development

| Stage | Description | Result/Output |
|---|---|---|
| Idea generation | Creation and databasing of ideas | New product proposal |
| Screening | Examination of ideas along pre-established criteria | Assignment of project team |
| Concept development, testing, and evaluation | Refinement of product concept, estimation of customer interest, augmentation of business analysis (financials), go/no go decision | Detailed product, market, financial and project plans; product specifications |
| Prototype development, testing, and evaluation | Physical development of product in R&D; functional and customer testing of the actual product | Final changes to product specifications and production plan |
| Pre-launch | Development of launch strategy; if necessary, market test or simulated market test; initial sales | Finalization of launch document; completion of product training, product support plans, sales collateral, and related written communications |
| Launch | Introduction and marketing of product as detailed in the launch strategy document | New-product launch |
| Project evaluation | Comparison of results to initial objectives | Suggested improvements for future projects |

ered for elimination as early as possible rather than investing more resources in their development.

During the concept development, testing, and evaluation phase, the team attempts to freeze product features and design specifications by collecting marketing research information, conducting quality function deployment (QFD), and/or developing engineering drawings. At the completion of this phase, the team should obtain approval from the new-product review committee for any capital expenditures required to build the prototype.

The prototype development, testing, and evaluation phase starts with the creation of a working model or preliminary version of the product. This model is then put through use tests either inside the company's facility or by customers. Alpha tests refer to having the product used by employees or a department in the company. Beta tests refer to having a select group of customers using the product under actual usage conditions. This phase could uncover potential defects that necessitate product elimination or redesign, or it may proceed to pre-launch scale-up and production planning. It's worth noting that although prototype development is presented after concept testing and development in this chapter, the reverse order is also possible. There are circumstances where customers cannot assess a concept in the abstract, such as when evaluating the taste of a new food product. In these situations, a prototype is required early in the process.

The pre-launch phase is the period of final preparation for commercialization. Product managers pull together details for the marketing plan, and engineering and production complete final product drawings and the debugging of tools. During the launch phase, the product is taken to the market, possibly through a planned roll-out. After launch, the new-product project is evaluated with a goal to either take immediate corrective action or to improve the process for the future. Each of these stages is described below, from the perspective of a typical product manager.

## Idea Generation

Although ideas can come from a variety of sources, both internal and external, the product manager should actively be looking for new-product concepts. Do not believe that there are already too many ideas. It is not just the number of ideas but also their quality that is important. The product manager is best suited to determine whether a flanker product is necessary to offset a competitive entry, or if a group of customers has adapted a product to a unique application that can be extended to other market segments. Subscribe to technological clipping services (either published or on-line) to monitor capabilities. Make customer visits to uncover different ways of thinking about the product category. Attend technology-sharing meetings (either within the company or through trade associations). Keep the information communication open with salespeople to identify opportunities. Monitor shifts in market size or composition that could suggest changing needs.

If there is no repository for product ideas in the company, create a database of ideas related to the product. Even ideas that didn't pass screening now may turn into winners in the future. Skim the database on a regular basis (perhaps quarterly or semi-annually) to determine whether any ideas should be dusted off and re-examined. (Refer to Chapter 7 for more information on idea generation.)

The output of idea generation will be a new-product proposal to be examined by the individual or group of individuals who determine whether to pursue new products. The new-product proposal will have the following components:

1. **Executive Summary:** A brief synopsis of the idea and proposed plan
2. **Present Situation:** The "fit" of the product into the strategic plan and a list of the problems and opportunities that triggered the concept
3. **Product Description:** The specific user benefits and advantages of the product along with how the product fits in the company's total offering, with photos, illustrations, or other techniques to make the concept more tangible
4. **Market Analysis:** An assessment of current and future market(s) for the product, competitive conditions and positioning, and any regulatory concerns
5. **Product Development Plan:** Any resources or technology required for the proposed product
6. **Marketing Plan:** The objectives and strategies for each area of marketing including pricing, distribution, advertising, sales, and product support
7. **Financial Analyses:** Projected cash flows and income statements and anticipated funds required
8. **Supporting documents:** Marketing research summaries or any other material that supports the project

## Screening

The second step of the product development process is screening. In this stage the product idea should be examined according to screening criteria established by appropriate company managers, including perhaps marketing, manufacturing, R&D, and senior management. Criteria can include things such as:

- Fit within existing product mix
- Patentability
- Risk of competitive entry
- Ability to sell through existing distribution
- Compatibility with strategic plan
- Acceptable paycheck period
- Growth potential
- Cost of tooling and machinery
- Compatibility with core technologies

The criteria for a specific company could include all of these or none of these. However, the act of listing them forces the issues to the surface and provides a forum for discussion of product concepts. The ideas that pass screening are prioritized, with project teams assigned as appropriate.

Many different approaches can be used for this process. Some companies simply indicate "must have" criteria for new products to be considered. Others list several criteria that can be evaluated on a yes-no basis. Still others use criteria with weights and ratings as shown in Figure 8.3. Note that the product idea being evaluated obtained a weighted score of 0.44. If several other ideas being evaluated simultaneously obtained scores of 0.56, 0.62, and 0.70, the relative priorities would become clear. The real value of these priorities is the ability to decide how to best allocate developmental resources.

A mathematical rating device such as this does not necessarily quantify results because the evaluations are still subjective. However, a screening checklist provides the opportunity for individual members to evaluate new-product ideas according to consistent parameters prior to meeting together as a group. It also fosters discussion among the new-product development review committee and focuses the conversation on aspects considered important to the company.

**Figure 8.3  Product Screening Checklist**

| Requirements for a Successful New Product | Relative Weight | (A) 0.0 | 0.1 | 0.2 | 0.3 | 0.4 | 0.5 | 0.6 | 0.7 | 0.8 | 0.9 | 1.0 | Rating |
|---|---|---|---|---|---|---|---|---|---|---|---|---|---|
| | | | | | | | Rating of Product Idea | | | | | | |
| Fit with existing product mix | .15 | | | | | X | | | | | | | .06 |
| Patentability | .05 | | | | X | | | | | | | | .02 |
| Low risk of competitive entry | .10 | | | | | | | | X | | | | .07 |
| Ability to sell through existing channels | .10 | | | | | | | | | X | | | .08 |
| Compatibility with strategic plan | .20 | | | | | | | | X | | | | .01 |
| Acceptable payback period | .10 | | | | | | | | | | X | | .09 |
| Growth potential | .10 | | | | | | X | | | | | | .05 |
| Low cost of tooling and machinery | .05 | | | X | | | | | | | | | .01 |
| Compatibility with core technologies | .15 | | | | X | | | | | | | | .05 |
| | | | | | | | | | | | | | .44 |

Whatever type of screening tool is used, it is important that it allow a reasonable balance between being too strict and too loose. A too-strict approach can cause potential winners to be killed. A too-loose approach results in mediocre products being pursued.

After the concept passes screening, a cross-functional team is established to work on the product. The team is usually comprised of the product manager and counterparts from operations, design, and, in some cases, procurement, legal, finance, customer service, and sales. The role of the salesperson will vary by company. Although sales input and upfront support are critical, not all salespeople can identify with the top 10 percent of potential or targeted customers that represent leading trends. A recent study by AT&T comparing salespeople's judgments with customers' judgments about an innovative new product concept found that the sales force was "consistently more optimistic and exhibited different preference patterns."[2] In that case, a rotating panel of salespeople is more appropriate.

## Concept Development, Testing, and Evaluation

The third step of the process is concept development, testing, and evaluation. It is an extension of screening, whereby good ideas are refined and elaborated to assess their financial, marketing, and technological feasibility. The process is progressive, starting out with secondary data and in-depth interviews with a small group of customers, then building to larger samples for more reliable estimates of market acceptance. Here the product manager is heavily involved in determining the appropriate features and attributes to maximize customer satisfaction and in estimating sales potential and profitability.

Concept development involves fleshing out the rough idea into a detailed product concept and expanding on the market size and attractiveness as presented in the initial proposal. Start with secondary data. Have a reference librarian (or the corporate librarian) conduct on-line searches to get more information on market characteristics, trends, and competition. Look for any purchasable marketing research studies that have been conducted on the market. If relevant, conduct patent searches to ferret out potential future competitors. Talk with industry experts and potential customers to assess attitudes toward the product idea.

Next, solicit input from key customers who are knowledgeable and cooperative. These customers don't have to be representative, but they do have to be willing to suggest improvements and modifications to the initial concept. Probe for specific modifications that could affect the sales potential of the product. What if certain features were enlarged? Minimized? What if the product were harder? Softer? What if the dimensions were more standardized? More customized? Is color important? How about location? Get as much input from these key informants as possible.

In some cases, this type of qualitative research with a small sample is sufficient to develop the concept. In other cases, a larger sample is required to fully understand needs. When the Oldsmobile Aurora was being developed, the project team used focus groups extensively even before the first designs were drawn. In fact, more than 4,200 consumers were interviewed nationwide—the largest such sampling in GM's history.[3]

Once the concept is more fully developed, it is important to test it among a large group of customers. This group will be more representative of the target market. There is no one best approach to concept testing, but most are variations of qualitative research and focus group discussions. Generally, several versions of a concept (possibly including competitors or placebo concepts) or several different product concepts that address the same need (i.e., substitutes) will be explored in one concept test. This is because people usually provide better information when comparing alternatives, and the resulting information is more reliable than absolute evaluation. Mock ads, product descriptions on cards, drawings of the concept, and rough prototypes can all be used as part of the research. In some cases, the product's technical documentation and owner's manual is part of this analysis.

Some of the questions to be addressed during the concept test include the following. Does the proposed concept make sense to the customers? Is it preferred over what is currently available? How much value do the improvements have over existing alternatives available to the customer? Is the product consistent with the way customers currently perform the function, or will it require a change in mind-set? Would they be willing to pay more? What are the flaws? Are there changes that would make the product viable (or more viable)? What is the basic need that this product would satisfy? Has the brand name or trademark been included in the concept test?

The concept tests usually include some indication of intent to buy at some specified price. "Intent to buy" refers to the respondents' indication of the probability they would buy the product if it existed, usually expressed along a scale (e.g., 1 = "definitely would not buy" to 5 = "definitely would buy"). This is an important component of the concept test but should not be projected literally as the actual sales potential. Customers will almost always overestimate their willingness to buy in an artificial setting such as a focus group. Obtaining pricing information is difficult at best. However, determining a target price is critical for establishing a target cost for the product development process. Although no research method is infallible, there are a few techniques that can be tried.

One tactic is to ask respondents what price they think would be competitively fair for the product as described, followed by a question on the likelihood to buy at that price. Another approach is to split the concept test groups into experimental and control groups. Give each group a different price for the same described concept and determine whether there are differences in the willingness to buy at the stated prices. A third strategy is to ask customers what value (in monetary terms) the new product would have over what they are currently using. A final approach is to ask customers what they would be willing to pay for the product and what features they would be willing to give up to attain that price.

At this step, the product team should attempt to establish a target price. The target price is necessary to estimate target costs for the developmental process. "Design by price" is an approach used by several companies in industries with rapidly changing technologies, short life-cycles and pressure on pricing.

> Compaq is a case in point. After being battered for several years by low-cost personal-computer rivals, Compaq struck back in 1992. It now builds computers that cost up to 60% less through what it calls "design to price."
>
> Here's how it works: a design team comes up with specifications for a new computer. It sits down with marketing, manufacturing, customer service, purchasing and other departments. Based on a price target set by marketing and a profit-margin goal from management, the team determines what the costs will have to be. To achieve cost targets, engineers design products with fewer parts and reuse parts from

existing designs. Compaq's factories have been overhauled to crank out products more cheaply and supplier contracts have been renegotiated, cutting material costs by $212 million in 1992 and $425 million [in 1993].[4]

The target price depends on the value perceived by the market. Determining value will be different for low-unit-value, frequently purchased items (e.g., consumer packaged goods) than for high-priced, infrequently purchased goods (e.g., capital equipment). The purchase of consumer packaged goods has an element of habit and inertia in the decision process. Higher-priced products may have groups or committees involved in the process. The differences in decision making, as well as the different decision makers, need to be included in the analysis.

Breakthrough products are the most difficult to value. Customers (whether consumers or industrial buyers) do not have competitive products to use as their benchmark price. Therefore, the analysis has to start with the function being provided by the product. How is that function being done now without the benefit of the new product or service? What benefits and costs are related to changing the way it is done now? Then both the rational and emotional motives for switching to the new product have to be considered and valued.

To estimate a target price, several things need to be considered, specifically the possibility of competitive attack, the price sensitivity of the market, and the degree of competitive differentiation. Figure 8.4 shows a tree diagram with the considerations in new-product pricing.

The appropriate technical people should be involved in the concept testing to assess the technological feasibility of any suggestions that customers might make. The concepts that appear to have mar-

## Figure 8.4  Considerations in New Product Pricing

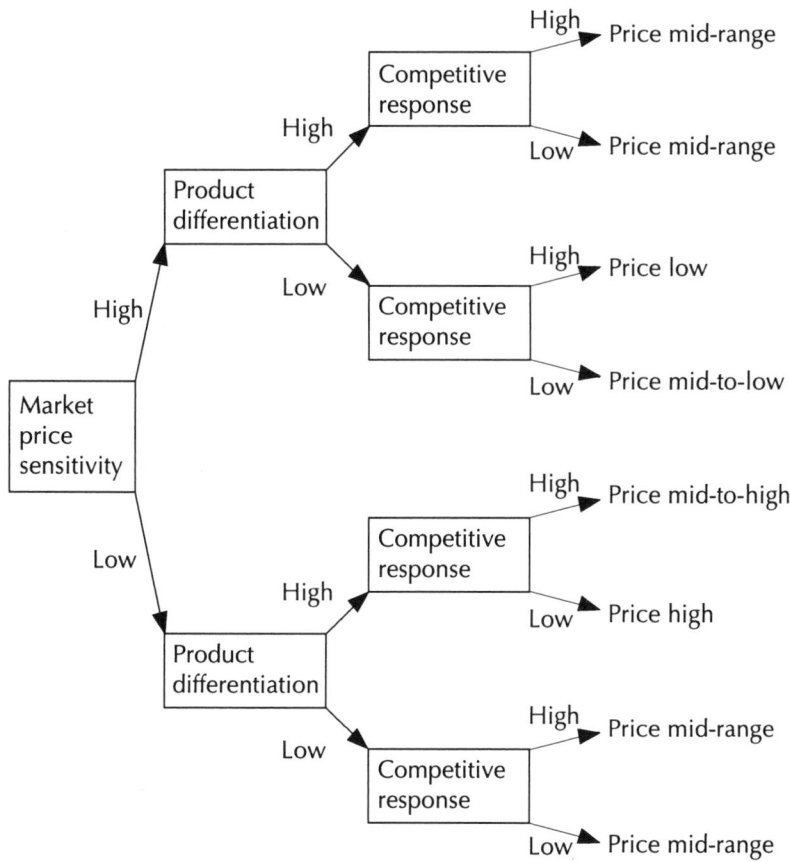

keting, technical, and financial feasibility are then subjected to a more detailed business analysis.

A rough business analysis will have been prepared prior to the idea screening (for the new product proposal) and it will have been refined concurrently with the concept testing. It should be continually evaluated and made more definitive as new information becomes available. At minimum it should be updated whenever a significant milestone has been reached. The skeleton proposal presented at the beginning of the process can now have some of the gaps filled in. The product description should now be more detailed, with marketing and cost objectives included. The market analysis should have more specifics on potential segments and niches, customer applications and key customer identification, and competitive benchmarks. The product development plan should include the composition of the project team, product specifications, a critical path chart with key milestones and target dates, and implementation schedules. The marketing plan should specify planned roll-outs, short-term and long-term resource requirements, identified risk factors, and suggestions for minimizing risk. The financial analyses should be expanded to include more detailed income statement and cash flow information than was available at the proposal stage. Figure 8.5 shows a simplified projected financial analysis for a hypothetical industrial product.

The revenue line is based on the market analysis and resulting forecast. The cost of goods sold is obtained from technical and manufacturing personnel on the product development team. The accuracy depends not only on their best assessment of per-unit costs, but also on the precision of the product manager's forecasts. The difference between the revenue and cost of goods sold is the gross margin available to cover fixed costs and contribute to profits.

The development costs include any costs already incurred for R&D and concept testing, as well as anticipated costs for prototype development, equipment and materials, labor, product testing, and additional marketing research. If the roll-out requires additional capital expenditures, they should be included here as well.

## Figure 8.5  Projected Financial Analysis

|  | Year 0 | Year 1 | Year 2 | Year 3 | Year 4 | Year 5 |
|---|---|---|---|---|---|---|
| Revenue | 0 | 10,700 | 13,843 | 17,689 | 25,428 | 29,242 |
| Less cost of goods sold | 0 | 3,583 | 4,635 | 5,923 | 8,515 | 9,792 |
| Gross margin | 0 | 7,117 | 9,208 | 11,766 | 16,913 | 19,450 |
| Development costs | −3,150 | 0 | 0 | 0 | 0 | 0 |
| Marketing costs | 0 | 7,200 | 5,814 | 7,430 | 10,679 | 12,281 |
| Allocated overhead | 0 | 1,070 | 1,384 | 1,764 | 2,543 | 2,924 |
| Gross contribution | −3,150 | −1,153 | 2,010 | 2,572 | 3,691 | 4,245 |
| Supplementary contribution | 0 | 0 | 0 | 0 | 0 | 0 |
| Net contribution | −3,150 | −1,153 | 2,010 | 2,572 | 3,691 | 4,245 |
| Discounted contribution (15%) | −3,150 | −1,003 | 1,520 | 1,691 | 2,111 | 2,110 |
| Cumulative discounted cash flow | −3,150 | −4,153 | −2,633 | −942 | 1,169 | 3,279 |

The marketing costs start at the pre-launch. These would include advertising, distribution, sales force coverage, sales promotion, and any miscellaneous selling and communication costs.

Allocated overhead refers to administrative costs allocated to various products. Some companies will assess a lower (or even no) overhead cost to new products until they have established themselves, while other companies believe that all products should provide an equal (or greater) contribution to fixed costs (i.e., a type of "hurdle"). Regardless of the company's attitude toward cost allocation, it is imperative that the estimated revenue (either price or number of units) is not artificially inflated simply to cover these costs.

The gross contribution is the amount of revenue remaining after development costs, marketing costs, and overhead costs are subtracted from gross margin. This is the amount of money that the product is expected to contribute to taxes and profit (if new-product sales have no effect on existing sales).

The supplementary contribution is used when new products have an effect (positive or negative) on existing products. The resulting cash flows should be included on this line and either added to or subtracted from the gross contribution to arrive at the net contribution. In Figure 8.5, gross contribution and net contribution were the same because the new product was not expected to have any impact on existing product sales.

The discounted contribution line shows the net present value of each net contribution figure, discounted at 15 percent per year. The last line shows the cumulative cash flows over time.

Before progressing to prototype development, it is important to revisit the questions that were used to evaluate the initial project and verify that it is still an attractive endeavor. This can be a critical milestone when another go/no-go decision must be made.

## Prototype Development

If the proposed product passes the concept test and evaluation, it moves into R&D and/or engineering to be developed into a physical product. Up until now it existed only as a verbal description or a rough mock-up. Now it must be translated into a technologically feasible product. This does not mean that marketing (or product management) is no longer involved. Rather, the product manager's job is to ensure that the core benefits that were the essence of the product concept are not lost during the development process and that progress is being made on the marketing plan, trade name search, and other factors critical to new-product success. That is why a project team approach is so crucial.

After the prototypes have been developed, they should be put to rigorous functional and customer testing. The functional tests are conducted under both laboratory and field conditions to be sure the products are safe and reliable (i.e., consistently perform as they are designed to perform). Customer tests are conducted to be sure that the design is appropriate. Market testing, in-home testing, and beta testing are all variations of the types of tests to be performed at this stage.

> Some manufacturers have built gigantic mechanical gizmos that can replicate almost any kind of abuse a product encounters. For example, a car takes a trip through Chrysler's huge climate-controlled lab where robotic drivers subject it to scorching heat and ice storms. Gerber recruits future customers of both sexes at birth and, with the help of enthusiastic parents, maintains a test panel of 2,500 toddlers through age 3.
>
> In order to make its PowerBooks even more customer-proof, Apple Computer puts all new models through common indignities. These include drenching them in Pepsi and other sodas, smearing them with mayonnaise, and, to simulate conditions in a car trunk, baking them in ovens at temperatures of 140 degrees or more.[5]

Some questions to be answered during this stage follow. Does the prototype work as intended? Does it meet specs? Does it satisfy customer needs? Are there any anticipated production problems? Can they be overcome within a reasonable time and cost? Has production scheduling been finalized? Is it on schedule? Have costs been confirmed? Have raw materials been ordered? Is marketing ready for launch? Are there minor modifications that can improve the product or its value without adversely impacting the project? Is there a need for a significant change that will necessitate a delay in the project?

If all these questions can be answered positively, the project is ready to move to the next stage: the pre-launch.

## Pre-Launch

The pre-launch is the period prior to commercialization when the product manager verifies that all preparations have been made for the actual product introduction. During this stage the product manager must identify all stakeholders and determine their information requirements. Customer service needs to be prepared to handle inquiries and fulfill orders. Technical support personnel may require specialized training. The distribution channel may require advance warning of any unique requirements of the product or service.

Also at this time there is a need to consider a market test or a simulated market test to determine whether the strategy (not just the product) is ready for introduction. Various use tests already should have determined the viability of the product, but the tests might not have addressed the best way to go to market. Test marketing helps assess whether the right price is being charged, whether the appropriate message is being communicated through advertising, and whether the proper distribution strategy is being employed. Of course, test marketing is expensive in terms of both money and time. Therefore, it should be undertaken only when the risk of *not* doing it is great.

For a typical test market, the product manager selects a geographic area that is as representative of the product's target market as possible and markets the product on a limited basis in that region. The key decisions to be made include how many test markets, which ones, and how long the tests should run. Most companies select two or three test markets that provide good representation of their target customers. Good representation refers to assuring that critical demographic variables are dispersed in the target area in about the same proportion as exists in the total market area. The length of the test market will vary depending on the type of product. Some will require 6-9 months and others will need two years. The factor to consider is the length of the buying cycle, with the test market being at least as long as two buying cycles.[6]

Based on this information, a launch plan can be developed. The launch documentation should contain three specific components: (1) a milestone activities chart; (2) the marketing strategy to support the launch; and (3) an early indicator chart. All of these guide the launch and early commercialization.

## Figure 8.6 Components of a Launch Control Document

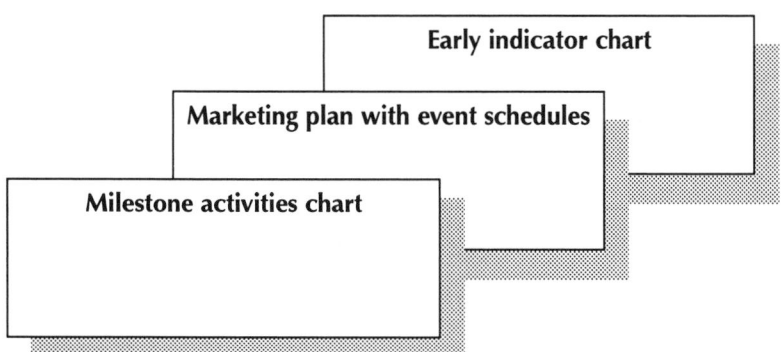

The milestone activities chart lists the desired dates of completion for various milestone activities such as purchasing equipment for the launch, finalizing package design, obtaining legal clearance, subcontracting specialized labor, preparing the owner's manual, etc. Each of these requires several steps and varies in importance depending on the project. Their potential impact on product success must be considered in assessing priority. For example, electronic or high-tech consumer products require clarity in technical documentation to be successful. Customers are increasingly seeking simplicity in a complicated world. However, as a recent *Business Week* article stated, "Plain English is a language unknown in most of the manuals that are supposed to help us use electronic products."[7] The format of the milestone activities chart can vary from a simple list of activities and dates to more formal project schedule and control techniques like Gantt and PERT charts. (Refer to operations management or project management books for more details.)

The marketing strategy component of the launch materials details the tactical components of the launch. Branding, packaging, pricing, advertising, and all aspects of marketing are studied. As with the annual product plan, the new-product marketing plan should start with an objective such as, "Convert 25 percent of current customers to the product upgrade and obtain trial by an additional 25 percent." The marketing tactics would then be put into place to accomplish this objective. A sample outline for this new-product marketing strategy is shown as Figure 8.7. Some companies include all or most of the listed components; others will need to be more selective. Line extensions might require only an abbreviated outline, whereas breakthrough products will need extensive marketing strategy plans.

## Figure 8.7 The Supporting New Product Marketing Plan

**A. New product objectives**
  1. Sales volume
  2. Market penetration
**B. Background summary**
  1. Total industry sales volume and trends
  2. Major competitors and analysis
  3. Market potential and segments
  4. Corporate charter
**C. The company's new product/ service**
  1. Product specifications/ description
  2. Brand name, trade name, and/or trademark
  3. Why is your product better?
  4. Main user benefits
  5. Customer profile(s)
  6. Primary selling points
  7. Positioning
  8. Potential barriers
  9. Frequency of purchase/use
**D. Entry strategy**
  1. Timing: When should the launch be planned?
  2. Roll-out sequence: What are the priority markets?
  3. Publicity
**E. Company support/preparation**
  1. Internal announcements
  2. Sales force tools
  3. Customer service training
  4. Technical support training
  5. Field seminars
  6. Policy statements
**F. Marketing plan**
  1. Product marketing objectives
  2. Target markets

  - New or existing customers
  - Demographics; psychographics
  3. Distribution
  - Channels of distribution
  - Markups/commissions/ other incentives
  - Available selling tools
  4. Pricing
  - Base price and discount schedule
  - Promotional pricing programs
  - Option pricing
  - Product line pricing
  5. Promotion
  - Sampling
  - Merchandising
  - Customer training
  6. Advertising
  - Product announcements
  - Press releases
  - Trade shows
  - User groups
  - Direct mail
  - Advertising (media and copy strategy)
**G. Cost and schedules**
  1. Development of sales support
  2. Training costs (including lodging and travel)
  3. Trade shows
  4. Media and advertising costs
  5. Sampling and merchandising costs
  6. Calendar of training schedules
  7. Media calendar
  8. Event schedule

A decision will need to be made whether to price a product high initially to recover the development costs or to price it low to gain market share faster. A number of factors affect this decision. First, how likely is it that competitors will enter the market soon? The ability of competitors to enter the market will be based on the investment required to enter, the ease of entering, and their own strategies. The faster that competition is likely to enter, the more appropriate a penetration (low) price strategy. Second, is there a large enough segment of customers willing to pay a high price for the product initially? Third, is the company, product, or service positioned appropriately for the price strategy being considered? Finally, what are the payback period, "hurdle rates," and return required by the company?

The final component of the documentation is the launch control plan. (See Figure 8.6.) The control plan will be developed from the milestone activities chart, the various event calendars and schedules from the marketing plan, and a calendar of early indicators of potential launch success. The first two components have been explained. The activities and target dates are listed and management control involves keeping the activities on track. The early indicators component requires a bit of explanation.

Early indicators refer to outcomes, such as the number of inquiries, that can help predict or provide early indicators of the level of launch success. For example, history might indicate that 30 inquiries typically convert to one sale. In that case, tracking the number of inquiries could provide an early indicator of future sales. Other early indicators might include the number of sales calls made on the new product, the percentage of distributors willing to carry it, the awareness level of the market, the number of facings retailers give to the product, etc. After identifying the early indicators, the next step is to set time-based (e.g., weekly, monthly) goals to achieve for each.

The early indicator chart, then, lists the outcomes expected by the end of designated time periods (e.g., each month), enabling the product manager to compare actual against expected performance without waiting for final sales data.

With launch documentation prepared, the product is ready to move to the launch phase of the product.

## Launch

The sixth step of the new-product development process, launch, results in the introduction of the product into the market. Decisions need to be made about timing (when to launch the product), geographic strategy, target market prospects, sales and customer service support, and final marketing strategy.

Timing can be a critical component of new-product success. If competitors might be (or are) entering the market, the product manager must decide whether to get there first, concurrently, or after the competition. First entry usually provides an advantage, but if rushing results in a flawed product, the result can be more damage than good. Timing an entry with competition can neutralize the competitor's potential first-mover advantage as well as possibly growing the potential market faster. Delaying an entry until after competition is in the market might make it possible to capitalize on competitive flaws as well as benefit from any competitive advertising that educates the market. Timing is also important if there are seasonal or cyclical aspects to a product or if the introduction impacts the sales of existing products.

It is also necessary to make decisions on a geographic strategy. On some occasions, a national launch is appropriate, but most new products start with a roll-out strategy. Prioritize the markets (e.g., regions, industries, or countries) and decide on an entry sequence. For example, it might be desirable to first enter the most attractive markets in terms of size and dollar potential. Or it might be more desirable to enter markets where competition is weak, providing an ability to gain experience, exposure, and market position. In other situations, the selection of roll-out markets is based on different product applications, pipeline inventory in the markets, ability to gain distributor or retailer support, company reputation in the market, or a host of other factors.

Although the roll-out might appear similar to test marketing, it differs in a couple of important ways. First, in a test market the product manager targets regions that are representative of the final launch. This is not the case with a roll-out. The markets are selected based on their ability to provide an early cash flow or to gain commitment from an influential market needed for the continued roll-out. Second, the test market is a final test before the commercialization decision is made. The roll-out is the first step in commercialization after the decision is made.[8]

As part of this geographic strategy, identify specific target market prospects. This is particularly important in the business-to-business market where clients/prospects can be listed by name. The more detail that can be provided here for the sales force, the greater the chances of encouraging them to sell the new product. That leads right into sales support. Work closely with the sales force to provide them with information that will help them sell. Prepare "how to sell it" booklets that discuss customers (not target markets), applications (not features), and useful questions to ask on a sales call. Make sure that customer service stays in the loop with sufficient communication through internal newsletters, informal and formal meetings, and various announcements.

The last part is fine-tuning of the introductory marketing strategy. This action plan details introductory pricing, base price, and option pricing; press releases and product announcements; direct mail to select customers; shipping policies and procedures; channel and end-user communications; and training for the sales force and/or customers.

## Project Evaluation

After (or during) launch some type of project appraisal should be completed. The main objectives of this stage are to improve future product development efforts and to move the product from a new-product to an ongoing product requiring long-term maintenance.

## References

1. Christopher Power, Kathleen Kerwin, Keith Alexander, and Robert D. Hof, "Flops," *Business Week,* August 16, 1993, 79.

2. Peter Strub and Steven Herman, "Can the Sales Force Speak for the Customer?" *Marketing Research* 5, no. 4, 32-35.

3. Kathleen Kerwin, "GM's Aurora," *Business Week,* March 21, 1994, 88-95.

4. Christopher Farrell, Zachary Schiller, Richard A. Melcher, Geoffrey Smith, Peter Burrows, and Kathleen Kerwin, "Stuck: How Companies Cope When They Can't Raise Prices," *Business Week,* November 15, 1993, 150.

5. Faye Rice, "Secrets of Product Testing," *Fortune,* November 28, 1994, 166-172.

6. C. Merle Crawford, *New Products Management,* 4th ed. (Burr Ridge, Ill.: Richard D. Irwin, 1994), 351.

7. Bruce Nussbaum and Robert Neff, "I Can't Work This Thing!" *Business Week,* April 29, 1991, 60.

8. C. Merle Crawford, *New Products Management,* 4th ed. (Homewood, Ill.: Richard D. Irwin, 1994), 351-353.

## Checklist: Keys to Successful New Product Development

✓ Know the market and what it needs.

✓ Select new products that play to a company's core strengths.

✓ Create a multifunctional project team early in the process.

✓ Get an early fix on costs and price.

✓ Get quality and price right the first time, even if it means delaying the launch.

✓ Build checkpoints into the system to make sure the developing product still meets the initial criteria under which it was approved.

✓ Do not introduce a new product simply to meet a new-product goal; be sure it fits the corporate strategy and customer requirements.

✓ Conduct alpha, beta, or market tests to gather user input.

✓ Include milestone activities and early warning indicators, along with relevant dates, in the launch control plan.

✓ Design a roll-out strategy to incrementally reach the best markets for the new product.

# Case Three

## The Many Aspects of Product Line Management

Product line management involves conceiving and developing new products, but also extending existing product lines and building brand equity. Different companies emphasize different parts of these product line management activities, and a given product manager will emphasize different aspects, depending on specific needs at the time. Examples of each are presented below.

### Developing New Products

In developing new products, product managers use a variety of techniques to reduce risk and increase chances of success. First, product managers (particularly in highly technical fields) have learned to begin next generation products immediately after the launch of prior generation products. Intel started this approach in 1990. Second, developing simultaneous products based on a corporate strategy leverages the success of both products by adding momentum. Intel demonstrated this as well with its ProShare family of products. Third, generating several products from a common platform spreads out development costs and allows products to be brought to market more quickly and at a lower price. Hewlett-Packard benefited from this knowledge in the introduction of its color Deskjet printer. Finally, establishing barriers to entry for the competition affords at least a temporary competitive edge. Here again, Hewlett-Packard discovered this in its work in inkjet printers.

### Intel's Next Generation Products

Companies are finding it necessary to bring out more products faster—particularly in high-tech fields. Intel, for example, has been picking up the pace of product development in the face of competition. It used to develop microprocessors sequentially, bringing them out about four years apart.

### Intel's Product Introduction Schedule

|                  | 286  | 386  | 486  | Pentium | P6   | P7        |
|------------------|------|------|------|---------|------|-----------|
| Start of design  | 1978 | 1982 | 1986 | 1989    | 1990 | 1993      |
| Introduction     | 1982 | 1985 | 1989 | 1993    | 1995 | '97 or '98 |

The sixth- and seventh-generation chips, on the other hand, were in process long before prior versions were introduced, with an emphasis on new applications and strategic alliances. Note that both the P6 and P7 were already under development when the Pentium was introduced. The P6 is focused on new applications, such as voice recognition and videoconferencing. The P7 is being designed under a new architecture with Hewlett-Packard. In 1994, an agreement was signed to meld Intel's traditional data-processing methods with H-P's reduced instruction set computing (RISC) technology.

To enhance the future launch of the P6 chip, as well as increase market potential for the Pentium, Intel developed and rolled out a new family of desktop videoconferencing products for PCs. This new family of products will enable computer users to work on the same document simultaneously over regular phone lines. The new development activities are consistent with Intel's vision of bridging the gap between communications and computer industries, as Tim Clark explains, in "Intel Sets $8 million Campaign," *Business Marketing:*

> Intel is positioning the new line as convergence products. "Along with our many partners, we are facilitating the conver-

gence of the communications and computer industries, turning the personal computer into a personal conferencing tool," [said] CEO Andrew S. Grove.

Working on simultaneous product platforms along with mutually beneficial product entries as Intel has done represents a couple of techniques companies have used to improve their product development processes. They've demonstrated the need to be proactive and plan strategically for new product development, as has Hewlett-Packard.

### Hewlett-Packard's Inkjet Printers

In an effort to maintain its dominance in printers, Hewlett-Packard has beaten Japanese competitors by using their own tactics. Over a decade ago Japanese companies had taken away the lead in hand-held calculators, a market H-P had pioneered. The success was due to a mass-market strategy with low-priced, well-designed products. This time H-P took that approach with inkjet printers, as Stephen Kreider Yoder explains in "How H-P Used Tactics of the Japanese to Beat Them at Their Game", *Wall Street Journal:*

> H-P engineers adopted two Japanese tactics: They filed a blizzard of patents to protect their design and frustrate rivals, and embarked on a process of continual improvement to solve the inkjet's problems. They developed print heads that could spit 300 dots an inch and made inks that would stay liquid in the cartridge but dry instantly on plain paper. One engineer tested all types of paper: bonded, construction, toilet—and, for good measure, added sandpaper, tortillas and socks.

Hewlett-Packard established a solid foothold in the black-and-white inkjet printer market using these techniques. However, it faced another challenge in 1990. At this time H-P engineers were working on a color printer, intent on bringing out a full-featured, mechanical marvel. Marketing suggested they build on the platform they had already established since they felt this approach, though less sophisticated, would satisfy the needs of the customers:

> There was a near mutiny among the engineers until a product manager named Judy Thorpe forced them to do telephone polls of customers. It turned out people were eager for the product the engineers considered a "kludge." H-P learned that "you can tweak your not-so-latest thing and get the latest thing," Ms. Thorpe says. By sticking to the existing platform, H-P was able to get the jump on competitors in the now-booming color-printer market.

One other thing: H-P's "blizzard of patents" set up a barrier to entry for competition. Competing engineers lost valuable time negotiating H-P's maze of 50 patents covering how ink travels through the head. By the time Canon became a serious competitor, H-P had sold millions of printers and had practiced continual improvement in manufacturing. Later, when Canon introduced a color inkjet in 1993, H-P was able to cut the price of its version before Canon even reached the market. As a result, Hewlett-Packard "owns" 55% of the world market for inkjets. And like Intel, H-P is leveraging its knowledge of inkjets in other areas such as fax machines. (See "Strategic Leveraging at 3M and Hewlett-Packard," page 146.)

### Extending Existing Product Lines—Successes and Failures

Sometimes products are not completely new, but rather they are product line extensions. As a product manager plans for line extensions, there must be a careful balance between variety and redundancy. Fast-moving consumer goods are perhaps particularly vulnerable to this trap. In an effort to respond to competitive entries, to reach smaller market segments, to bolster short-term gain, and/or to gain more shelf space, many product managers offer variations of core products to reach finer segments.

Numerous examples abound. When Nabisco introduced its line of Fat Free Fruit Bars in 1993, the cookie category was growing at a modest 2 percent per year. Nevertheless, this line of offerings resulted in Nabisco's sales increasing three times as fast as the overall market. Similarly, when 7-Up introduced Cherry 7-Up in 1987, the new product variant was successful and the sales of the core product also went up.

Unfortunately there are pitfalls to line extensions. Introducing a product variation under the same name as a core brand could have the potential of weakening the brand equity. Line extensions can generally be easily matched by competitors. A number of hidden costs could arise due to increased production complexity, more errors in forecasting, and the loss of consumers due to potential out-of-stock situations.

As an example, John Quelch and David Kenny, in the *Harvard Business Review* ("Extend Profits, Not Product Lines") discuss the plight of a U.S. snack foods company they refer to as Snackco. Over time, Snackco's product line had grown, but its overall sales remained flat. In evaluating the situation the company studied the effectiveness of core products, niche products, seasonal and holiday products, and filler products. The percent of the line as well as the percent of the sales volume accounted for by each type of product are shown in the table "Snackco's Product Line Analysis."

## Snackco's Product Line Analysis

|                      | Percent of line | Percent of sales volume |
|----------------------|:---------------:|:-----------------------:|
| Core products        | 20%             | 70%                     |
| Niche products       | 10              | 10                      |
| Seasonal and holiday | 5               | 10                      |
| Filler               | 65              | 10                      |

By looking at this analysis it was clear changes had to be made. Note that the core products generally followed the Pareto principle: 20 percent of the products accounted for 70 percent (instead of Pareto's 80 percent) of the volume. These were also the key products responsible for building company and brand reputation. Consequently, Snackco managers changed manufacturing and delivery schedules to assure that core products were always in stock.

The niche products were holding their own, contributing 10 percent of the product line and 10 percent of the volume. These products were studied to determine in which market areas they had sufficient volume to continue, and in which markets they should be dropped.

Seasonal and holiday items provided 10 percent of the sales volume even though they represented only 5 percent of the product line. These items were maintained with additional store displays provided for active selling periods.

Finally, filler products were evaluated. Even though the per-unit contribution was greater than for some of the other products, it wasn't enough to offset the fact that with 65 percent of the product line they were contributing only 10 percent of the sales volume. These products were carefully evaluated in terms of true costs and competitive need. The company decided to cut the number of filler products. The greatest cuts were in competitive areas where the company decided to use the shelf space to build share in core products. In leadership markets, the cuts were more selective with a goal of blocking shelf space from the competition.

Note the steps that Snackco took to perform this analysis. First, the *sales/profit/contribution* history of each of the items in the product line were collected and analyzed, along with data on customers and competitors. Part of this was based on internal records. But to be able to fully *evaluate product performance,* external research was also required. Random store checks indicated that the most popular items were out of stock up to 50 percent of the time and that up to 40% bought either a competitive product or nothing. The rest purchased one of the filler products. The company also used consumer tracking panels to gain data on both household purchases and usage frequency.

After examining this information, Snackco managers were challenged to *add value to existing products and to the product line,* particularly for retail channel members. As Quelch and Kenny point out, they had to be able to prove that retailers would benefit from the product line plan being proposed:

> Snackco's managers believed that the new strategy was on target, but they also knew that without the support of the sales force, any efforts to implement the plan would fail. So, backed by Snackco's president, one of the sales regions undertook a four-month test to determine the impact of refocusing core products versus continuing line extensions. Not only did market share increase during the test, but sales-force compensation also increased because of the faster turnover of the more popular items in the line, which were given additional shelf space at the expense of the slower-moving items.

To *boost market penetration,* usage rate and/or the number of users had to be increased. Some of this was accomplished by scheduling manufacturing and delivery to assure that core products were always in stock, as well as providing additional store displays for the seasonal products. However, some advertising changes were also necessary:

Snackco shifted from an umbrella advertising approach for the whole line to a strategy that focused on its flagship products. Advertisements for these products emphasized the Snackco brand and thereby promoted the brand's line extensions. Over the past two years, Snackco has made significant gains in market share and volume, which in turn have generated even higher margins.

Source: Adapted from: Robert Hof, "Intel: Far Beyond the Pentium," *Business Week*, February 20, 1995, 88-90; Tim Clark, "Intel Sets $8 Million Campaign," *Business Marketing*, February 1994, 1, 40; John Quelch and David Kenny, "Extend Profits, Not Product Lines," *Harvard Business Review*, September-October 1994, 153-160; Stephen Kreider Yoder, "How H-P Used Tactics of the Japanese to Beat Them at Their Game," *Wall Street Journal*, September 8, 1994, 1+.

# SECTION FOUR

# FUNCTIONAL SKILLS

The core product or service is only part of the "package" a customer buys. Price, brand reputation, purchase convenience, and other factors influence the success of a product.

Therefore the product manager has to be competent in dealing with these marketing support aspects of the product. Price must balance company costs and profitability with customer satisfaction. The product manager must be aware of the financial costing of the product, the impact of price concessions, typical aspects of price sensitivity, potential competitive reactions, and the need to consider channel members in pricing decisions.

Marketing communications can provide favorable or unfavorable, strong or weak, consistent or inconsistent messages to the market. Careful monitoring is required to determine the best trade-offs among various advertising vehicles, sales collateral materials, trade shows, seminars, and sales promotion techniques.

Also, the method used to go to market might need to be changed or at least refined. As distributors and retailers gain more knowledge of and influence with end-users, product managers need to cultivate them to assure product success.

This section highlights the marketing skills necessary for a successful product line. Special attention is devoted to pricing and marketing communication decisions and activities.

# 9

# PRICING PRODUCTS AND SERVICES

An important part of a product manager's marketing function is pricing a product to balance profitability and customer satisfaction. For existing products, the eight-step process described in this chapter provides the basic considerations for setting prices and making price changes. The eight steps involved in setting price are as follows:

1. Determine corporate strategy and position
2. Identify the role of price in achieving the position
3. Evaluate costs related to the pricing decision
4. Estimate the price sensitivity of the target market(s)
5. Anticipate competitive actions and reactions
6. Assess potential legal consequences (if appropriate)
7. Calculate profit implications
8. Incorporate price changes/implementation in the product plan

## Determining Corporate Strategy

The first step, determining corporate strategy, should have been accomplished in the business assessment (Worksheet 4.1). The corporate direction might specify a premium position or a mass-merchandiser/discount approach. These obviously have direct impact on the pricing. If a product is a cash cow, is being used to enter a new market, or requires a specific ROI, that is necessary knowledge in setting price. On the other hand, in a decentralized organization, the corporate position might have minimal impact on product planning and price will play a neutral role.

Avoiding price wars might be part of a corporate pricing strategy. For many companies, this can be done only by reducing the cost of producing products, as H.J. Heinz Pet Products chief Bill Johnson found out. After facing intense price pressure from the competition, Johnson decided that meeting price cuts, without also lowering the internal cost structure, would be deadly.

> "We decided to run pet foods assuming the price war would never end," he says. To do so he turned the pricing equation on its head. "Instead of calculating out what it cost to make cat food and price accordingly, we asked ourselves what did consumers want to pay," Johnson explains. His team decided that today's finicky customers would pay between 25 cents and 33 cents per 5 1/2-ounce can, tops. Johnson then went to work rationalizing processes to hit that target. Step one was identifying his company's competitive advantages, to wit, strong brand equity, cheap materials in the form of excess tuna from Heinz's StarKist operations—which goes into more than 15% of Pet Foods' products—and some proprietary manufacturing processes. "Step two," says Johnson, "was a draconian reduction of cost."[1]

## Identifying the Role of Price in Achieving Position

What role can price play in achieving the corporate goals? Think about how other companies and industries price their products and develop an idea file of pricing approaches. Here are a few examples to start an idea file:

- **No-haggle pricing:** Offering a set price in an industry known for "negotiation." Currently being used by Saturn and Ford Escort in the automotive industry.
- **Always the low price:** Charging a constant low price rather than using frequent promotions. Used at the retail level by Wal-Mart and at the manufacturer level by Procter & Gamble.
- **Step pricing:** A discount policy in which prices are reduced for set quantities in a step-wise fashion. For example, one price for 1-100 units, a reduced price for 101-300 units, a still-lower price for 301+ units, and so forth.
- **Price point pricing:** Setting price points across a product line to denote quality differences. Many consumer products are priced this way, using a "good-better-best" approach in terms of quality. Structure the prices so that customers are most likely to buy the highest-profit product in the line. Sometimes it is preferable to introduce a lower-priced variation than to reduce the price of a core product. (See "Zebra Technologies Fights Price Competition with No-Frills Product.")
- **Peak-time pricing:** Charging a higher price for peak-period usage and a lower price for non-peak times. Phone companies, utilities, and movie theaters routinely use this approach.

- **Bundled pricing:** Creating a "package" of features or products and selling the bundle for one price. Car companies use this approach with their option packages.
- **Unbundled pricing:** Taking packages apart and selling components individually. Many products in the mature phase of the product life-cycle use this approach, allowing customers to select and pay for specific features only. Unfortunately, customers frequently attempt to start with the low price of a main component and negotiate inclusion of free features, reducing the effectiveness of this technique.
- **Trial pricing:** Charging a low price for new products or new customers to encourage trial of a product.
- **Quantity discount pricing:** There are several variations of this technique. Companies can charge a reduced price for a given quantity per order, cumulative quantities over a fiscal year, or some combination.
- **Cross-connected pricing:** Allowing a discount on one product/service when purchasing another. Commonly used among airlines, car rental firms, and hotels.
- **Leasing:** Paying a time-based fee (e.g., weekly or monthly) for the right to use a product. Used increasingly in the automotive industry as an alternative to purchasing the vehicle.

## Evaluating Costs

Evaluating the costs related to the pricing decision is often more difficult than it seems. Companies use different approaches for allocating costs, so the variable and fixed costs can become blurred. Nevertheless, definitions of these common pricing terms are relevant.

Variable costs are those that vary (in total) with production of the product or service. This could include direct materials and labor. For

---

# Zebra Technologies Fights Price Competition with No-Frills Product

Zebra Technologies Corp., a Vernon Hills (Ill.) maker of bar-code printers, had developed a reputation among customers as a manufacturer of high-quality, top-of-the-line printers. But the company also saw a lot of sales potential in the low-end portion of the marketplace. A low-priced, low-frills printer was a cinch to make. But offering such a model posed two risks: It might tarnish Zebra's image of quality with its customers, and, worse, it might cannibalize the existing product line.

The solution? Zebra came up with a no-frills version with a plastic housing that pleased its clients. But it didn't give away the store: It made sure that the stripped-down $1,495 printer couldn't be upgraded to ensure that it wouldn't compete with its high-end $1,995 model, which is faster and can print on different kinds of materials. The result: The new Stripes printer helped Zebra's sales climb 47 percent last year, and margins on the new printer match those from Zebra's original line.

Source: David Greising, "Quality: How to Make it Pay," *Business Week*, August 8, 1994, 58.

---

a given production level, these are constant per unit and provide the floor for pricing decisions. Fixed costs do not vary with production or sales; they exist whether or not the product is even produced. Fixed costs can be allocated according to square feet of production space, percentage of a product's contribution to total revenue, split equally among product managers, or a variety of other approaches. In the long run **all** costs must be covered, and the long-term pricing of products should consider all costs. However, in the short run, any price obtained that exceeds variable costs can at least contribute to fixed overhead and (potentially) profit.

Variable costs will often be equal to the cost of goods sold and be the only incremental costs relevant to a pricing decision. There are exceptions when fixed costs are incurred for a bid situation, for example, that are incremental to that decision. In that case the incremental fixed costs must be added to the variable costs to determine the floor for pricing decisions.

This information should be reflected in an income statement. A simplified income statement contains the following:

|  | Sales |
|---|---|
| Less | Cost of Goods Sold |
|  | Gross margin |
| Less | Operating Expenses |
|  | Selling expenses |
|  | Marketing expenses |
|  | Administrative expenses |
|  | Net operating income |
| Less | Other expenses |
|  | Net income |

Fixed costs can include the fixed costs directly attributable to a product line as well as other allocated costs. The fixed costs directly attributable to a product line would be the operating expenses for that product. Subtracting these from the gross margin yields the operating income a product manager provides. Other allocated costs would be subtracted from this figure to arrive at net income.

The following break-even formula can be used as a starting point for evaluating a price. The standard break-even formula shows the number of units that must be sold at a given price to cover all costs. The formula is:

$$\text{Break-even units} = \frac{\text{Fixed costs}}{(\text{Price} - \text{Variable cost per unit})}$$

Therefore, if relevant fixed costs are $20,000, the product has a price of $300, and variable cost per unit is $110, it would be necessary to generate sales of 105 units just to break even. By experimenting with different price levels and matching that with expected demand, the product manager can begin the pricing analysis. In addition, a target return (profit) can be included in the numerator (along with fixed costs) to assess the unit sales necessary to contribute a specified profit. For example, if a required profit of $10,000 were added to the fixed costs in the numerator, it would be necessary to generate sales of 158 units to break even.

This formula can also be adapted to look at the impact of a price change. The modified formula is shown below. *CM* stands for contribution margin; when cost of goods sold includes all incremental, avoidable costs, contribution margin is the same as gross margin. The % *CM* refers to the contribution margin per unit expressed as a percentage of the price. The result is the percentage change in unit sales necessary to contribute the same profit return as now.

$$\% \text{ break-even sales change} = \frac{-(\% \text{ price change})}{(\% \text{ } CM + \% \text{ price change})}$$

Building on the previous example, assume that current projected sales are 2,000 units, resulting in projected revenue of $600,000 ($300 × 2,000 units). What would be the change in break-even sales if price were cut by 5 percent? The % $CM$ = ($300 – $110)/$300, or 63 percent. Therefore:

$$\% \text{ break-even sales change} = \frac{-(-.05)}{.63 + (-.05)} = .086 = 8.6\%$$

To compensate for a 5 percent price cut, it would be necessary to increase unit sales by 8.6 percent or 172 units just to be generating the same return as now. This same answer can be obtained by using the formula to generate a spreadsheet for the relevant contribution margins and cost change variables, as in Figure 9.1.

What would have been the necessary change if the variable costs were lower so that the contribution margin was 70 percent, with everything else equal? In this case, it would have been necessary to increase sales by only 7.7 percent, or 154 units, to break even. What if variable costs were significantly higher so that the contribution margin was only 40 percent? Again, with everything else the same, what sales change would be necessary to break even? Now the answer is 14.3 percent, or 286 additional units.

Price increases also can be evaluated by using Figure 9.1. However, if a price increase is necessary, it can be useful to time the increase with a product change or additional service that adds value.

So in looking at price changes, it is necessary to understand what impact those changes have on required volume to break even, and then ask a couple of questions. How much leverage do competitors have? If their variable costs on this product are lower, they would be able to withstand a price cut longer. How likely is it that they would want to cut price and sustain it? Also, how sensitive are customers to price changes? Is it possible to sell the required volume change?

# Figure 9.1 Spreadsheet Example of Break-Even Analysis of Price Changes

| Price Change (%) | Contribution Margin | | | | | | | | |
|---|---|---|---|---|---|---|---|---|---|
| | 0.65 | 0.60 | 0.55 | 0.50 | 0.45 | .040 | .035 | .030 | .025 |
| 0.10 | −0.13 | −0.14 | −0.15 | −0.17 | −0.18 | −0.20 | −0.22 | −0.25 | −0.29 |
| 0.09 | −0.12 | −0.13 | −0.14 | −0.15 | −0.17 | −0.18 | −0.20 | −0.23 | −0.26 |
| 0.08 | −0.11 | −0.12 | −0.13 | −0.14 | −0.15 | −0.17 | −0.19 | −.021 | −0.24 |
| 0.07 | −0.10 | −0.10 | −0.11 | −0.12 | −0.13 | −0.15 | −0.17 | −0.19 | −0.22 |
| 0.06 | −0.08 | −0.09 | −0.10 | −0.11 | −0.12 | −0.13 | −0.15 | −0.17 | −0.20 |
| 0.05 | −0.07 | −0.08 | −0.08 | −0.09 | −0.10 | −0.11 | −0.13 | −0.14 | −0.17 |
| 0.04 | −0.06 | −0.06 | −0.07 | −0.07 | −0.08 | −0.09 | −0.10 | −0.12 | −0.14 |
| 0.03 | −0.04 | −0.05 | −0.05 | −0.06 | −0.06 | −0.07 | −0.08 | −0.09 | −0.11 |
| 0.02 | −0.03 | −0.03 | −0.04 | −0.04 | −0.04 | −0.05 | −0.05 | −0.06 | −0.07 |
| 0.01 | −0.02 | −0.02 | −0.02 | −0.02 | −0.02 | −0.02 | −0.03 | −0.03 | −0.04 |
| −0.01 | 0.02 | 0.02 | 0.02 | 0.02 | 0.02 | 0.03 | 0.03 | 0.03 | 0.04 |
| −0.02 | 0.03 | 0.03 | 0.04 | 0.04 | 0.05 | 0.05 | 0.06 | 0.07 | 0.09 |
| −0.03 | 0.05 | 0.05 | 0.06 | 0.06 | 0.07 | 0.08 | 0.09 | 0.11 | 0.14 |
| −0.04 | 0.07 | 0.07 | 0.08 | 0.09 | 0.10 | 0.11 | 0.13 | 0.15 | 0.19 |
| −0.05 | 0.08 | 0.09 | 0.10 | 0.11 | 0.13 | 0.14 | 0.17 | 0.20 | 0.25 |
| −0.06 | 0.10 | 0.11 | 0.12 | 0.14 | 0.15 | 0.18 | 0.21 | 0.25 | 0.32 |
| −0.07 | 0.12 | 0.13 | 0.15 | 0.16 | 0.18 | 0.21 | 0.25 | 0.30 | 0.39 |
| −0.08 | 0.14 | 0.15 | 0.17 | 0.19 | 0.22 | 0.25 | 0.30 | 0.36 | 0.47 |
| −0.09 | 0.16 | 0.18 | 0.20 | 0.22 | 0.25 | 0.29 | 0.35 | 0.43 | 0.56 |
| −0.10 | 0.18 | 0.20 | 0.22 | 0.25 | 0.29 | 0.33 | 0.40 | 0.50 | 0.67 |

# Estimating Price Sensitivity in the Target Market

The fourth step is estimating the price elasticity of the target market(s). Although there are some research-based techniques for estimating price sensitivity, conducting this type of research is at best difficult. As a starting point, begin with a managerial assessment, asking the following questions:

- How strong is the product positioning, its differentiation in the customers' eyes? Is the differentiation based on an important, relevant characteristic? *(The stronger the differentiation and the more important it is perceived by the customer, the less sensitive to price the customer is likely to be.)*
- Is there a lot of competition? Are customers aware of the competition? Can customers find substitute ways of fulfilling the same need without buying any product? *(The fewer options the customer has for providing the same benefit(s) as a product provides, the less sensitive to price the customer is likely to be.)*
- What was the impact on sales when there were price increases/decreases in the past? Consider both internal and competitive price changes. *(If prices were raised in the past without a significant loss to the competition, the less sensitive to price the customer is likely to be.)*
- Is the product part of a larger purchase? *(The smaller the product purchase is as a percentage of a larger purchase, the less sensitive to price the customer is likely to be.)*
- Is the product a capital expenditure or an expense item? *(The less expensive the absolute price of the product, the less sensitive to price the customer is likely to be.)*

After completing the managerial assessment, research might be necessary to gather more specifics. Here is some of the information that would be beneficial. What are the highest and lowest prices that fall within the customer's relevant range? What does price mean to the customer? Is the absolute or comparative price more important? Are they considering shipping and operating costs as part of the price? Part of this analysis should include a search for new products and markets where price is less important. (See "Using Innovation to Reduce Price Competition.")

Remember that a market can be multi-level. If the product is sold to as well as through intermediaries such as distributors, dealers, and retailers, the price charged has to consider them as well. First, price so that their margins will be large enough to motivate them to do what they need to do. Second, consider how the margins they add affect the price the end-users ultimately pay. Third, corporate and pricing positions have to be consistent with image of the channel member. Finally, use the spreadsheet you created from the break-even sales equation (Figure 9.1) to begin setting the discount structure for the channel.

## Anticipating Competitive Actions and Reactions

The fifth step requires a look at the competition. First of all, how do the prices compare with the major competitors? What benefits do the products provide that have perceived value to the customers? It is useful here to try to put a monetary value/cost on the differences between the product and its competitors. Much of the information will be subjective, but it still forces evaluation of the cost/benefit analysis more carefully. Start with the competitor's price, then add and subtract internal estimates. (See Figure 9.2.)

Part of the competitive analysis should also include what actions competitors might take in response to a price change. Any records of competitive responses to price changes in the past will be a valuable starting point. In highly competitive industries, companies use pricing strategies actively to preempt competition. This is the approach Intel took with the Pentium chip:

---

## Using Innovation to Reduce Price Competition

As always, one way to exit a price war is to innovate. Take Becton Dickinson's hypodermic needles. The company produces over a billion each year, at a paltry dime apiece, worth over $100 million in sales. Prices have been flat to down over the past decade. During one particularly painful period in the late 1980s, a Japanese competitor began selling its wares for 7 cents a unit. In other words, you would not want to be stuck in the needle business. Then Becton Dickinson got together with Baxter International, which had developed InterLink, a needleless needle.

The point to remember is that the needles doctors stick in your arm account for about 50% of the market. The other half are used to hook up intravenous lines to other IVs, which is where the Baxter-Becton team made its mark. InterLink looks like a regular syringe except the needle is replaced by a hard piece of tapered plastic tubing that ends in a blunt tip. Baxter created a new type of plastic-and-rubber seal that could be punctured and then would reseal around such a plastic spike. Baxter asked Becton to produce the spike.

Hospitals gladly pay more for InterLink because the pointless needles lower the risk of accidental needle sticks. [In 1993] health care workers reported about one million sticks, costing hospitals upward of $400 per incident in lost time and paperwork, excluding any legal or long-term health costs. "That's the attraction," says Gary Cohen, a marketing VP with Becton Dickinson. "Even though InterLink needles cost about 25 cents, hospitals save money."

Source: Andrew E. Serwer, "How to Escape a Price War," *Fortune,* June 13, 1994, 90.

---

With a 90% share of the microprocessor market, Intel Corp. could be forgiven for putting up its feet for a while. Instead, the $8.8 billion chipmaker has startled rivals by launching an unprecedented price war. Over the next three months, it plans to cut prices on everything from mainstream 486 chips to top-of-the-line Pentiums—leaving some products 40%

## Figure 9.2 Estimating Monetary Value of Competitive Differences

| | | | |
|---|---|---|---|
| Competitor's price | | | $5,000 |
| Value of added benefits | | | |
| Monetary savings | | | |
| Longer life | $500 | | |
| Lower failure rate | 250 | | |
| Labor savings | 1,000 | | |
| Total Savings | 1,750 | | |
| Monetary costs | | | |
| Switch-over costs | –500 | | |
| Economic value to the customer | | 1,250 | |
| (The $1,250 is a best estimate of the true "worth" of differences between the product and the competition. It should be added to the competitor's price to arrive at the economic or financial value to the customer.) | | | |
| Incentive to switch | | 750 | 500 |
| (The $750 is the amount subtracted from the economic value to make the product more attractive and provide an incentive to switch.) | | | |
| Your price | | | $5,500 |

cheaper than just four months ago. A growing pack of hungry rivals is out to steal a chunk of Intel's wildly profitable, $7 billion, IBM-compatible, PC microprocessor business. . . . Intel's strategy: Outrun them all. By slashing prices fast, it hopes to establish Pentium as its mainstream chip by mid-1995—before rivals can make much of a showing.[2]

## Assessing Legal Consequences

The Sherman Anti-Trust and the Robinson-Patman Acts are the two pieces of legislation most relevant to pricing decisions. The Sherman Act (along with amendments of the Clayton Act) prohibits practices that reduce competition or inhibit trade. Collusion or price fixing is one such practice. Companies may not legally collude with competitors to set prices (horizontal price fixing) and they may not require channel members to charge certain prices (vertical price fixing).

The Robinson-Patman Act prohibits certain forms of price discrimination. In general, it is illegal to sell "products of like grade and quality" at different prices to competing resellers if the result is to restrain trade.

## Calculating Profit Implications

The seventh step demonstrates the bottom-line impact of the prices and price changes—typically in the form of a profit and loss (P&L) or income statement. Some companies that use a cost-plus-markup approach want to see the impact of price changes on a per-unit basis. This is appropriate when there is a relatively low number of high-ticket sales. However, for most products the impact of a markup can be deceiving if forecasted sales are not taken into account. If there are several products in the line or multiple price combinations, it is useful for planning purposes to present all of this information in an impact table, perhaps using a spreadsheet format. (See Figure 9.3.)

## Incorporating Price in the Product Plan

The last step in pricing is to incorporate pricing into the marketing plan. Do not forget that several internal customers (e.g., customer service, sales, other product managers) must be informed of the approved changes. Also, some pricing strategies might require additional promotional material, changes in packaging, or other things

## Figure 9.3  Price Change Impact Table

|  | Product 1 | | | Product 2 | | | Product 3 | | | Total |
|---|---|---|---|---|---|---|---|---|---|---|
|  | Price A | Price B | Price C | Price A | Price B | Price C | Price A | Price B | Price C |  |
| Sales Units |  |  |  |  |  |  |  |  |  |  |
| Revenue |  |  |  |  |  |  |  |  |  |  |
| Cost of goods sold |  |  |  |  |  |  |  |  |  |  |
| Gross margin |  |  |  |  |  |  |  |  |  |  |
| Total gross margin |  |  |  |  |  |  |  |  |  |  |
| Operating expenses |  |  |  |  |  |  |  |  |  |  |
| Operating income |  |  |  |  |  |  |  |  |  |  |
| Other expenses |  |  |  |  |  |  |  |  |  |  |
| Net income |  |  |  |  |  |  |  |  |  |  |

Note: The "Total" column provides the basis for the income statement in the annual product plan.

that could affect the marketing plan. Finally, if a price change is being tested in a certain region or for a certain period of time, be prepared to track the results for making future decisions.

## References

1. Andrew E. Serwer, "How to Escape a Price War," *Fortune*, 13 June 1994, 84.

2. Robert Hof, "Fortress Intel," *Business Week*, 22 August 1994, 28.

## Checklist:  Pricing Products and Services

✓ Forget everything you know about how pricing is done in your business. The best new ideas you can get are from outside your industry.

✓ Avoid raising or lowering prices simply in response to competition or internal costs. Assess how your customers might respond to the change and determine whether this reaction justifies the change.

✓ Consider a no-frills product variation as an alternative to price cutting when faced with competitive pressure.

✓ Time your price increases with added value.

✓ Understand the contribution margins of all products in your line, and the impact that has on pricing decisions.

✓ Conduct a managerial assessment of how sensitive your target market is.

✓ Innovate and look for new product-market segments where price sensitivity is lower (and your product will be able to obtain a higher price).

✓ Anticipate competitive reactions before making price changes.

# 10

# THE PRODUCT MANAGER AS MARKETING MANAGER

Marketing encompasses a multitude of activities involved in getting a product to the right market at the right time and at the right price. Since the product manager is ultimately responsible for this, it is critical that marketing services (e.g., advertising, marketing research) and distribution strategy not be ignored. Making sure that the right competitive position is established is the starting point for the development of an effective strategy.

How is the product/service different from the competition? This can be a tricky question, particularly for commodity products like mortgages. However, Arbor National Mortgage, a midsize company in Uniondale, New York, has developed a positioning approach that has worked. By repackaging a standard mortgage into a bridal registry, the result was a distinctive identity.

Arbor takes a standard Fannie Mae mortgage and repackages it into the Arbor Home Bridal Registry. Couples register with Arbor instead of a department store so friends and families can contribute to the newlyweds' first home. "Running the registry is a lot of work, so we aren't as concerned with getting couples to register as we are in getting inquiries about purchasing a first home," says Boyles [Arbor's senior vice president of marketing]. "Only three dozen couples have actually registered but we've had over 5,000 couples call about the service. Their names are now in our database. We hope to have them as customers someday." Arbor also holds mortgage seminars for real estate brokers, accountants, and consumers. And the company plants a tree for customers who want one, either in their yard or in a public forest.[1]

Product managers shepherd this process through a variety of functional areas and are responsible for communicating the appropriate messages to the target market(s), setting a price consistent with the value provided, and evaluating the distribution activities to ensure superior end-customer satisfaction. The previous chapter examined pricing considerations. This chapter looks at the advertising, distribution, and various support components of the marketing function.

## Marcom Planning

The marketing communications portion of the product plan addresses the setting of the advertising objectives, media planning, and creative strategy. In some cases, publicity, telesales, and/or sales support will be part of the plan. This is the direction of "integrated marketing," tapping into the potential synergy of all communication vehicles. Product managers will usually be more interested in direct response activities than in purely image or corporate advertising. Even consumer marketers are becoming increasingly involved in database marketing, with the aim of targeting messages more effectively and measuring the response to the investment in advertising.

### Setting Objectives

The starting point for the advertising plan is the setting of objectives. The statement of objectives would follow the same format as the overall marketing objective. It would include *what* to communicate *to whom* and with *what results*. Should the advertising generate sales, produce leads, or enhance an image? To whom must the message be communicated to make that happen? What will be the result of this communication? $X$ revenue? Number of leads per prospect reached? A percentage change in awareness? If the product manager runs a mail-order operation with no sales force, it might be appropriate to have an objective of generating $X$ sales from a defined target market over the next 12 months. But most companies would have some combination of sales, lead generation, and/or image reinforcement.

If the product is not sold directly to the end-user, a decision must be made about what part of the budget will be devoted to advertising to the end-customer (a pull strategy) and what part will be devoted to trade advertising (a push strategy). These two groups will require different media and different messages.

After deciding what to communicate to whom and with what results, the next question is *how* to make it happen. That is the essence of the advertising plan: deciding on the media and creative strategy. Although much of the detail work will be handled by the company's advertising department or through an advertising agency, the product manager needs to understand the basics to make good

# Database Marketing

A growing number of marketers are investing millions of dollars to build databases that enable them to figure out who their customers are and what it takes to secure their loyalty. In 1992, for example, General Motors Corporation joined with MasterCard to offer the GM Card. As a result, GM now has a database of 12 million GM cardholders, and it surveys them to learn what they're driving, when they next plan to buy a car or truck, and what kind of vehicle they would like. Then, if a cardholder expresses an interest in, say, sport-utility vehicles, the card unit mails out information on its truck line and passes the cardholder's name along to the appropriate division.

Blockbuster Entertainment Corporation is using its database of 36 million daily transactions to help its video-rental customers select movies and steer them to other Blockbuster subsidiaries. In Richmond, Virginia, the company is testing a computerized system that recommends 10 movie titles based on customer's prior rentals. The suggestions are printed on a card that also offers targeted promotions. Customers who have rented children's films, for example, might get a discount at Discovery Zone, Blockbuster's playcenter subsidiary.

Source: Jonathan Berry, John Verity, Kathleen Kerwin, and Gail DeGeorge, "Database Marketing," *Business Week,* September 5, 1994, 57.

evaluative decisions. The media planning will consist of: (1) listing potential media, (2) selecting appropriate media vehicles, (3) assessing trade-offs, (4) examining media combinations, and (5) developing a media calendar. The creative strategy converts the positioning and unique selling features into effective customer communications.

## Media Planning

Media planning starts with selecting the appropriate media and media vehicles to accomplish the stated objectives. Decide how many to use (to increase reach) and how often to advertise in each (to increase frequency). Then coordinate resources to get maximum return from the investment in advertising. That means it is sometimes necessary to violate traditional turf boundaries that separate the media (including boundaries between marketing and sales) and focus on the intended results (objectives) of the advertising.

**List Potential Media** Start by developing a list of all media and promotional methods that could be used to accomplish the objectives. Analyze each according to editorial format, circulation, frequency, and cost. Then prioritize the list according to each medium's ability to contribute to the plan's effectiveness. The larger the potential audience, the more a product manager will need to consider broad-reach media. The smaller the audience, the more targeted the media must be.

The primary media choices for consumer communications are listed in Figure 10.1. It is not a comprehensive list. It is simply intended to trigger a few ideas for thinking through the media options. The primary media choices for a business target market include some of the consumer media choices but go beyond as well. (See Figure 10.2.)

# Figure 10.1  Consumer Media Considerations

| Category | Some "Best" Uses | Rate/Cost Considerations |
|---|---|---|
| **Print** | | |
| Newspapers | ▪ Ads that don't require high print quality<br>▪ Local coverage of all demographic segments<br>▪ Inserts<br>▪ Coupons | ▪ Agate line or colum inch rates<br>▪ ROP (run of paper)<br>▪ Color rates<br>▪ Insert rates |
| Magazines | ▪ Demographic selectivity<br>▪ Color print quality | ▪ Page rates (or fractions of)<br>▪ Color rates<br>▪ Bleed rates<br>▪ Cover rates |
| **Broadcast** | | |
| Radio | ▪ High frequency<br>▪ Auditory messages<br>▪ Appeal to specific demographics | ▪ Dayparts (e.g., drive time)<br>▪ ROS (run of station)<br>▪ Local, spot, network |
| Television | ▪ Mass coverage<br>▪ Impact of sight and sound<br>▪ Short message (except for infomercials) | ▪ Daypart (e.g., prime time)<br>▪ Specific programs<br>▪ Local, spot, network |
| **Direct mail** | ▪ Direct response<br>▪ Identified audience<br>▪ Long message | ▪ List rental<br>▪ Postage rates |
| **Publicity** | ▪ "Newsworthy" events<br>▪ Credibility | ▪ Personnel/time costs |
| **Miscellaneous** | | |
| Outdoor | ▪ Frequency<br>▪ Mass local audience | ▪ Poster size<br>▪ Traffic count |
| Transit | ▪ Frequency | ▪ Inside/outside/station posters |
| Point-of-purchase | ▪ Stimulate impulse buying | ▪ Retailer negotiation |

## Figure 10.2 Business Media Considerations

| Category | Some "Best" Uses | Rate/Cost Considerations |
|---|---|---|
| **Print** | | |
| Newspapers | ■ Frequency (compared to trades)<br>■ For select markets where newspapers are significant | ■ Agate line or column inch<br>■ ROP (run of paper)<br>■ Preferred position<br>■ Color rates (if available) |
| Trade journals | ■ Product appeals to specific reader profile<br>■ Product can benefit from image of journal | ■ Page rate (or fraction of)<br>■ Color rates<br>■ Preferred position |
| General business publications | ■ Need to reach a broad mix of influencers or decision makers | ■ Same as above |
| Consumer publications | ■ No trade reaches your market<br>■ You can afford the additional impressions even at the expense of wasted coverage | ■ Same as above |
| Directories | ■ Purchasing agents play a role in the sale | ■ Ad size |
| Card decks | ■ Low-cost products | ■ Number of inserts |
| **Broadcast** | | |
| Television | ■ Large target market<br>■ Corporate or image advertising | ■ Selected programs |
| Radio | ■ Primary market concentrated in limited geographic areas<br>■ Frequency | ■ Daypart<br>■ ROS (run of station)<br>■ Local, spot, network |
| **Direct mail** | ■ Identified audience<br>■ Lead generation or direct sale | ■ List rental<br>■ Postage rates |
| **Sales literature/brochures** | ■ To advance the sales call | ■ Print charges |
| **Catalog** | ■ Reference material | ■ Print charges |
| **Trade shows** | ■ Demonstration of product | ■ Booth charges<br>■ Direct and indirect labor |
| **Publicity** | ■ "Newsworthy" events | ■ Direct and indirect labor |

**Select Appropriate Vehicles** Second, select the most appropriate media vehicles. A message of quality is best carried in a publication that is a "bible" of the industry, whereas announcements of new industrial products are better placed in new-product digests. For product managers not working through an agency (either internal or external), some preliminary information on the media vehicles can be obtained from Standard Rate & Data Service directories available at libraries with business collections. From that information, the product manager can estimate the cost per prospect for each media vehicle. After narrowing the list, request media kits from the rest to obtain more specific information on reader profiles, frequency discounts, ability to obtain reduced list rental with a paid ad, and information about the effectiveness of advertising in the specific publication or broadcast medium.

**Assess Tradeoffs** Third, assess the tradeoffs between the size (cost) of the ad, the impact on prospects, and the number of times it can be placed. The cost of a large ad is more than the cost of a smaller ad. However, because a large ad is seen (noted) by more people, the cost per person noting the ad can provide more efficiency. The assessment should also include placement within the medium. For magazines, ads on the inside covers, the front part of the publication, adjacent to specific editorial content, and/or isolated from other advertisements usually have the most effectiveness. For radio, drive-time spots typically reach more people than ROS (run of schedule). For television, news has the greatest audience size, although specific programs might have a closer match to the target audience. For direct mail, odd-sized and dimensional mailings can have more impact, but they increase the cost, thereby limiting the potential reach and frequency of the mailings. In general, with a given budget, it is usually better to increase frequency at the expense of reach rather than to increase reach at the expense of frequency.

What is the necessary frequency of communication to maximize response? That depends on several things. Messages promoting a unique product or having a unique format require less frequency to be noticed than "commodity" ads. The more advertising messages a person is exposed to at one time (e.g., within one publication), the greater the number of insertions required to break through the clutter. The more complicated the message or the less differentiated, the more likely it is that more than one impression will be required to be effective.

**Examine Media Combinations** Fourth, examine combinations of media that could increase effectiveness. This is the "synergy" part of integrated marketing. For example, timing a telemarketing sales call right after the intended receipt of a direct mail piece can increase the response. Using different media simultaneously can sometimes break through the target market's perceptual barriers. This approach increases frequency, but different media can also increase *reach* by appealing to different segments of the market or to different influencers or decision makers. Making decisions on reach versus frequency and continuous versus pulsing advertising strategies is part of this analysis. Figure 10.3 provides a checklist of considerations for making the decisions.

**Develop Media Calendar** Finally, after examining costs and benefits of the various media types and combinations, put the entire media plan into calendar format for the year. (See Figure 5.4.) This accomplishes two things. First, it forces the product manager to think in advance. Second, by seeing the combinations of media in one place,

## Figure 10.3  Setting Media Objectives

| | Objectives | | | |
|---|---|---|---|---|
| | Reach | Frequency | Continuity | Pulsing |
| **Message needs** | | | | |
| New or highly complex message,strive for | | * | | |
| Dogmatic message, surge at beginning, then | * | | * | |
| Reason-why messages, high frequency at first, then | | | | * |
| Emotionally oriented messages | | | * | |
| When message is so creative or product so newsworthy they force attention | * | | | |
| When message is dull or product indistinguishable, strive for | | * | | |
| **Customer purchase patterns** | | | | |
| To influence brand choice of regularly purchased products | | * | * | |
| As purchase cycle lengthens, use | | * | | * |
| To influence erratic purchase cycles, strive for | | * | | * |
| To influence customer attitudes toward impulse purchases | | * | * | |
| For products requiring great deliberation, alternate | * | * | | |
| To reinforce consumer loyalty, concentrate on | * | | * | |
| To influence seasonal purchases, anticipate peak periods with | * | * | | |
| **Budget levels** | | | | |
| Low budget, use | | | | * |
| Higher budget, strive for | | | * | |
| **Competitive activity** | | | | |
| Heavy competitive advertising, concentrate on | | * | | |

## Figure 10.3, continued

| | Objectives | | | |
|---|---|---|---|---|
| | Reach | Frequency | Continuity | Pulsing |
| When competitive budgets are larger, use | | | | * |
| **Marketing objectives** | | | | |
| New product introductions to mass market | * | | | |
| To expand share of market with new uses for product | * | | | |
| To stimulate direct response from advertising | | * | | * |
| To create awareness and recognition of corporate status | * | | * | |

Source: Courtland L. Bovee and William F. Arens, *Contemporary Advertising* (Burr Ridge, Ill.: Richard D. Irwin, 1982), 469.

the potential impact they have on each other can be improved. Third, the calendar helps focus on integrated marketing communications by incorporating nontraditional communications vehicles (e.g., seminars, newsletters, and software programs) into the plan. (See "Red Star Adopts Integrated Marketing Communications Programs.")

### Creative Strategy

The creative strategy should include the basic message and positioning that should be communicated to the target market. Although an advertising agency might be responsible for the creative design of the advertising, the product manager should at least be able to critique it. As mentioned earlier, the advertising message depends on the positioning statement developed at the start of the planning process. The message should always be consistent with the positioning or unique selling proposition (USP) and include customer benefits that differentiate the product from the competition. Sometimes a company is interested in being positioned as innovative and uses patents to

---

## Red Star Adopts Integrated Marketing Communications Program

In the early 1990s, Red Star Specialty Products discovered that the messages reaching its trade customers were inconsistent. Their market of food technologists didn't know how Red Star products were different from competitors' products. Worse yet, only 10 percent of those responding to trade ads were "A" leads and 70% were "C" leads.

Since Red Star's $300,000 marketing budget could not be increased, it had to reevaluate where and how it spent its promotional dollars. First it scaled back its trade ads and used some of the money for educational materials, such as brochures, newsletters, and seminars. Another educational tool Red Star developed was an interactive software program with a tutorial on flavor enhancers and a guide to using specific products. These helped position Red Star as an advisor to food companies that had slashed their own R&D staff.

The company also developed an improved database to more effectively reach customers and prospects. According to Marketing Manager Tim Roebken, "Before, the most we had done is work with an industry magazine and do a direct mail piece to their list of subscribers. It was still a wasteful, mass-advertising approach. Of the 30,000 subscribers there may have been 5,000 or 6,000 we wanted to reach."

By examining problems and opportunities and acting on a specific positioning strategy, Red Star was able to increase the effectiveness of its marketing communications without increasing its total budget. The difference is that now two-thirds of the marketing budget is devoted to new vehicles (with only $100,00 spent on advertising), and all are integrated to provide a consistent message to the market.

Source: Adapted from Joe Mullich, "Red Star Crafts a New Marketing Recipe," *Business Marketing,* December 1994, 6+.

---

"prove" that position. Titleist has used its patented dimpling process to "prove" the quality of its golf balls; Samsonite luggage uses line drawings depicting patents and patents pending for the various product features.[2] In any case, the objective of the advertising is to convince potential customers that your product is different from the competition in an important way and that this difference is strong enough to motivate them to buy.

For print advertising, the headline should attract prospects to the ad. Sometimes this can be done by stating the benefit or the promise of a reward. At other times, a provocative question will be more successful. The headline should generally maintain a positive tone and be coordinated with the rest of the ad. The copy should contain a benefit in the lead paragraph and use present tense, active voice words. If the copy is long, use subheads to make it easier on the eye. Identify what the prospect is to do as a result of reading the ad. Most business advertising (and a growing amount of consumer advertising) strives for direct response, so the copy should include the 800 number or other contact information. The layout should take eye movement into account and have a single dominant element rather than being overly cluttered.

For broadcast advertising, hold the number of elements to a minimum. Words should be conversational, using concise copy. Take advantage of impact if using television commercials. With radio, be sure the company/product name is mentioned often.

For direct mail, set up repeated tests. Test different copy, different package formats, and different mailing lists. If possible, have a control to test against an alternative for each mailing. Personalize the cover letter and talk about the prospect's needs—not about the product. Use a strong offer to encourage people to respond. Do not simply encourage them to contact the company for more information; provide an incentive such as a free booklet, reduced price, trial offer, etc. If using direct mail (or any direct response advertising) be sure to have inquiry fulfillment materials available. Highlight on the envelope that this is the information the prospect requested.

Include the salespeople in evaluating direct response lead generation programs. Let them see it before it is mailed to customers and prospects, and ask them for input. Not only will salespeople offer useful suggestions, but also they will be more likely to buy into a program if brought in at the early stages.

### *Evaluating Advertising Effectiveness*

Regardless of the medium used, collect as much data as possible on the return generated by each (return on promotional investment, ROPI). This will help determine which media are most effective and help in future budgeting. If advertising is done for long-term image reasons, periodically conduct image surveys to determine whether the investment is being well spent.

## Sales Promotion

In addition to advertising, product managers might be involved with a variety of other promotional techniques, such as sampling, sales contests, and various other incentive programs. These are referred to as "incentive programs" because they provide incentives to stimulate short-term incremental sales of the product as opposed to building long-run brand loyalty. Promotions are commonly used to introduce new products, influence the effectiveness of competitors' tactics, or tap into a new market.

Product sampling can be an effective technique for encouraging customers to try a new product. New products that require behavioral change by potential users generally benefit from the ability of customers to try them on a low-cost or no-cost basis. 3M's Post-It Notes, for example, required free sampling for customers to experience using the product. Test drives are a method of sampling in the automotive industry. Rent-with-the-option-to-buy is a form of sampling that reduces cost (and risk) to both parties.

## Distribution Strategy

Unless a product manager's products are distributed differently from all other products in the company, chances are that he or she will not have significant control over strategic methods of distribution. Most of the activities will be related to working with the existing distributors, dealers, or agents and perhaps expediting shipments as necessary. However, some new products will necessitate changes in the channel of distribution, or market and competitive forces will require changes for existing products. This could also be a critical element of the plan if a product manager is rolling out a product into new regions and/or expanding globally. As a result, distribution strategy should not be ignored as the product manager develops the annual marketing plan.

Whenever a product manager introduces a lower-priced or higher-priced product, or one that has a different image, it might be neces-

sary to introduce new channels. A potentially successful product can
be thwarted by the wrong channel decision, as Huffy found when it
introduced its new Cross Sport bike.

> Huffy Corp., for example, the successful $700 million bike
> maker, did careful research before it launched a new bicycle
> it dubbed the Cross Sport, a combination of the sturdy
> mountain bike popular with teenagers and the thin-framed,
> nimbler racing bike. Huffy conducted two separate series of
> market focus groups in shopping malls across the country,
> where randomly selected children and adults viewed the bikes
> and ranked them. The bikes met with shoppers' approval. So
> far, so good. In the summer of 1991, Cross Sports were
> shipped out to mass retailers, such as the Kmart and Toys 'R'
> Us, chains, where Huffy already did most of its business.
> That was the mistake. As Richard L. Molen, Huffy president
> and chief executive explains the company's slipup, the
> researchers missed one key piece of information. These spe-
> cial, hybrid bikes, aimed at adults, and at $159, priced 15%
> higher than other Huffy bikes, needed individual sales atten-
> tion by the sort of knowledgeable salespeople who work only
> in bike specialty shops. Instead, Huffy's Cross Sports were
> supposed to be sold by the harried general salespeople at mass
> retailers such as Kmart. Result: "It was a $5 million mistake,"
> says Molen. By 1992, the company had slashed Cross Sport
> production 7% and recorded an earnings drop of 30%.[3]

As markets fragment, different target customers—even for the
same product—might seek alternative channels of distribution. Key
accounts, for example, might best be served by going direct, whereas
other customers can be more efficiently served through distributors.

On the other hand, small customers might be handled by telesales, even if there are outside reps calling on larger customers in the same territory. Specialized distributors or agents might be more successful with certain segments than existing intermediaries, and that possibility should be periodically explored.

Effectively motivating intermediaries can have a positive impact on the bottom line for the products. This starts by keeping a careful record of distributor or rep activity by product and assessing overall capabilities. Product managers should accompany regional or sales managers in routine visits to distributors or reps and might be expected to help prepare joint marketing plans. If there is an advisory council, the product manager should review the meeting minutes (at minimum the sections related to his or her product line) and react accordingly.

Manufacturers' and resellers' goals do not always match. Product managers sometimes tend to view resellers as the destination of their product. Resellers, on the other hand, view the receipt of a product as the beginning of a sales cycle. This can create unnecessary conflict, which can be reduced by a better sharing of information.

Product managers spend a good deal of money and effort to understand end-user needs and how their products fit these needs. Resellers should also be given this information. Providing this education to resellers not only helps them work better, but also enables them to provide valuable feedback to the manufacturer on product performance.

## Product Support

Product support can encompass several things: installation, warranty follow-through, product upgrades, repairs, customer training, etc.

The product manager might not be directly involved with these activities, but he or she should be concerned about whether the policies and procedures are in place for them to happen. Customer satisfaction frequently depends as much on these factors as it does on the product itself. In addition, the product manager might be involved in developing services that optimize profit potential from various segments. We will examine some of the product support issues that a product manager might want to handle operationally or include in the marketing plan.

The cost of installation can be included in the price of the product or be an "optional" or unbundled component. The decision should be made in conjunction with the appropriate personnel (e.g., the service manager). If any significant changes are to be made, they should be mentioned in the marketing plan, with the impact on other marketing activities and on the bottom line.

A warranty or service contract can affect the salability of a product and should be examined along with other features. There are several questions to consider here:

- What do customers expect?
- Will there be a full or limited warranty?
- Can competitors match the warranty? Will they?
- Should the warranty be handled by the manufacturer, by the dealer, or by an independent organization?
- What are the advantages and disadvantages of service contracts and extended warranties?

As with any other part of the action program, changes to be implemented to the support program during the next fiscal year should be included in the marketing plan along with the impact and rationale.

## Marketing Research

After completing the action program portion of the marketing plan, there will likely be information gaps that will require more data before the next planning cycle. This could include formal survey or focus group research, on-line database searching, and/or analysis of internal customer records and databases. If so, it is a good idea to include these activities as action items in the marketing plan to assure that resources and approvals have been attained. When a major project is expected, solicit proposals prior to the development of the action plan so that the time or cost of the project is not underestimated.

## References

1. Andrew Serwer, "How to Escape a Price War," *Fortune,* 13 June 1994, 88.

2. W. David Gibson, "Going Off Patent: Keeping the Wolves from Your Door," *Sales & Marketing Management,* October 1990, 76-82.

3. Christopher Power, "Flops," *Business Week,* 16 August 1993, 79.

## Checklist: Marketing Your Product

✓ Don't limit your marketing budget to advertising the same way you always have. Test new approaches and techniques.

✓ Be sure your communications reach the right people. It's better to have an average ad with a direct hit than a terrific ad shown to the wrong people.

✓ Experiment with database marketing to pinpoint the right message for the right customers.

✓ When creating print ads, strive to have a benefit or a reward in the headline.

✓ Integrate your marketing communications techniques to increase their effectiveness.

✓ Consider sales promotions as part of your marketing communications toolbox.

✓ Don't automatically assume that your current method of distribution is best for your product or that it won't require a change in the near future.

✓ Match the capabilities of your distributors or retailers with the selling requirements of your product.

✓ Monitor and control product support as a potential value-added component of your product.

# 11

# PRODUCT MANAGEMENT: THE FINAL FRONTIER?

Product management has been evaluated, criticized and applauded since its first introduction. Several writers have questioned whether product management will be a premier organizational structure in the future or whether it has become obsolete. Brand management, the most common form of product management in consumer goods companies, has perhaps come under the heaviest attack for several reasons. The availability of market data is unprecedented, causing brand managers to become overwhelmed. At the same time, senior managers demand more data to justify marketing decisions in the face of growing competition and a saturated market demand. Brand managers are being put under more scrutiny, with more and more decisions requiring higher management approval before progress can be made. Disillusionment with the system is high.

In other industries where product management has had a shorter history, the function is being viewed as a functional solution to several organizational problems. In particular, the approach is being implemented to provide the necessary match between the market's needs and the firm's ability to translate its core capabilities into products that satisfy these needs.

Regardless of the industry, product management is, and will continue to be, a viable organizational form. However, there will be modifications. Three variations to the original product management structure will likely play a role in the future for several companies. These variations—product management teams, more specialized focus, and a business unit manager approach—will be discussed in this chapter.

## Product Management Teams

The use of product management teams (PMTs) to make product-related decisions has surfaced recently, possibly spurred by the reengineering craze. The specific role of the team, as well as its effectiveness, it still unclear. To put PMTs into perspective, it is useful to look at the evolution of teams in corporate America over the past decade or two and to provide some general categorization of teams.

The widespread use of teams started in the 1980s with the growth of quality circles, used primarily in the auto and steel industries to combat Japanese competition. In general, workers and supervisors met intermittently to discuss quality problems and did provide suggestions for *incremental* improvements. However, they rarely provided breakthrough thinking and began to lose their appeal. Nevertheless, the interest in teams continued, with the groups evolving into either worker-teams or project teams:

> The teams most popular today are of two broad types: work teams, which include high-performance or self-managed

teams, and special-purpose problem-solving teams. Problem-solving teams, in particular, differ from quality circles in important ways. Where quality circles are permanent committees designed to handle whatever workplace problems may pop up, problem-solving teams have specific missions, which can be broad (find out why our customers hate us) or narrow (figure out why the No. 3 pump keeps overheating). Once the job is done, such teams usually disband.

While problem-solving teams are temporary, work teams, used by about two-thirds of U.S. companies, tend to be permanent. Rather than attack specific problems, a work team does day-to-day work. A team of Boeing engineers helping to build a jet would be [an example of] a work team.[1]

The differences between the structure of the two types of teams are also worth noting. The project teams are frequently cross-functional, comprised of individuals representing the various operative areas related to the specific mission of the team. The work teams, although occasionally multifunctional, are more likely have members who are similar in job function, with the authority to make decisions about how daily work is done.

The trouble with some PMTs being created today is that they combine the two structures, in effect developing an ongoing cross-functional team without a specific mission, yet without the ability to make decisions on daily workloads. This isn't meant to imply that teams cannot exist within a product management structure. Nevertheless, a product manager should be prepared to work with *numerous* problem-solving teams on an ongoing basis rather than one ongoing team.

Teams will be critical in product deletion decisions, issues related to establishing a consistent corporate image among all products in the company, work flow and scheduling, and new product development. These teams will likely have different members and different time-periods involved. The product manager will take on the role of integrator across these teams as they relate to the product line in question and will be responsible for managing a bundle of projects at different stages of completion.

The company will also play a role in assuring that the various teams work together. If teams have to build consensus among both functional and team bosses, as at DEC, great time can be lost. On the other hand, empowering problem-solving teams to make immediate decisions can be both motivating and time-saving.

> [DEC announced in July 1994] it was abandoning its matrix team structure. Under the old system, workers in functional areas—engineering, marketing—also served on teams organized around product lines like minicomputers or integrated chips. The teams spent endless hours in meetings trying to build a consensus between the two factions in the matrix: the functional bosses and the team bosses. Its sheer organizational weight left DEC a laggard in the fast-moving technology sector.
>
> Boeing has an organizational structure similar to DEC's but with a critical difference. Its structure encourages teams to work together and seize initiative. Says Henry Shomber, a Boeing chief engineer: "We have the no-messenger rule. Team members must make decisions on the spot. They can't run back to their functions for permission." This kind of freedom allowed Boeing to use teams to build its new 777 pas-

senger jet, which flew its first successful test flight this summer [1994] with fewer than half the number of design glitches of earlier programs.[2]

## More Specialized Focus

Given the growing responsibilities assigned to product managers, some companies are questioning whether there is simply too much for one individual to handle. As a result, there has been movement toward narrowing the focus of the product manager. The type of focus is company-or industry-specific. A number of fast-moving consumer-goods (FMCG) companies, for example, have split the position into two areas of specialization. One manager focuses on consumer issues and the other on trade issues. Del Monte followed this type of reorganization in 1993. "The intent is to become more of a specialist," said Christine Di Fillippo, brand manager of tomato products at Del Monte.[3]

The ability to deal with the trade is likely to continue to escalate in importance. Although retail giants have existed for a long time, their clout has increased due to the emergence of powerful information systems that provide them with more data on consumers than manufacturers have. Consumer-goods manufacturers are finding it necessary to organize around their customers (the retailers), invest in technology, and act more as a partner than was typical in the past. Vendors to Wal-Mart have to respond to a barrage of demands to get their product sold (or even on the shelves). Companies are also increasingly including retailer input at the early stages of product development. Black & Decker solicited input from several retailers, including Home Depot, when it introduced the DeWalt line of power tools. The president of Black & Decker's power tools group emphasized their involvement: "We talked to them about the name. We talked to them about the color. We talked to them about the warranty."[4] Their input was valuable not only in terms of product design, but also as a visible sign of their involvement as a partner.

Other FMCG companies have restructured to allow the brand manager to focus more specifically on product issues, with advertising handled under a corporate umbrella. There is some logic to this approach when a company brand identity is more important to the market than the brand image of the line or item over which the product manager has control. However, unless the product has unique technical demands, the position of product manager might not be necessary in this situation, and a functional organization could suffice.

Some highly technical companies have taken a similar route, having product managers focus on the engineering and technical aspects of a product, with most marketing decisions handled by a separate function. In this case the product manager may become a technical/applications expert with the job of helping the salespeople, while the other individual is responsible for understanding the market and communicating product benefits to them. The risk of separating marketing from development is that the product manager loses contact with the customer and becomes too close to the product to be objective.

Whatever attempts are made at specialization to make the product manager's job more manageable, it's critical to remember why the position was created in the first place: to better understand the product and its competition so that customer needs are satisfied.

## Business Unit Manager

Other companies have reorganized into what are essentially business units, with the product manager responsible for the general management of the product line. This is a type of team arrangement that elaborates on the PMT concept but in a sense allows a more specialized focus on the product as a business. Under this type of structure, the product manager assumes more responsibility for *all* of the business functions related to the product, going well beyond the marketing and planning.

> While the product manager has always worked in a spectrum ranging from marketing specialist to general manager, the business unit structure places greater emphasis on the general management side.
>
> Jennifer Kan at Specialty Brands is part of this new kind of team and has new responsibilities over areas such as finance and inventory. "Companies seem to be searching for the next generation of organizations, trying to figure out what will work best in the upcoming years," she said.[5]

If product managers are to be held fully accountable for the success of their products, it's reasonable to expect them to be given sufficient authority to make that happen. The business unit manager structure affords the format to make it possible. However, it also requires that the person hired for the position have the experience, reputation, and respect to carry it out.

## Other Trends

There are at least two trends likely to impact the future of product management, particularly in larger firms. One is the growth of global megabrands. The other is the dramatic metamorphosis of distribution channels and logistics management.

The globalization of brands is occurring in both consumer and business arenas. Kelly Services, a temporary worker agency, has both domestic and international locations. Coca-Cola, Sony, and Levi Strauss are brand names recognized throughout the world. Companies are realizing they have to accept this movement toward global brands as inevitable.

> Major brand companies frequently inform the media that globalization is their most pressing challenge. The year 1990 saw a series of acquisitions and (more commonly) mergers because companies felt the need to expand in order to compete in a global market: Hoffman La Roche and Genetic or Merck and Du Pont in pharmaceuticals; AT&T and NCR in computers; Matsushita and MCA in entertainment electronics; Whirlpool and Philips in white goods; Asahi and Elders IXL in beer. Procter & Gamble's chairman Edwin L. Arztz offered these words at the company's general meeting in 1990: "The acquisition strategy will be driven by globalization, which will be the principle engine of growth in sales. It's not optional. That's the way business will be done."[6]

What does this mean for product managers? Many product managers will be challenged to understand market needs for their products beyond American borders. The transition for some companies will be minor if few changes are required to the product or its marketing. In other cases, extensive marketing research, product adaptation, and promotional modifications will be unavoidable. The product manager may also be required to work with company personnel located at plants or offices in other countries, sometimes coordinating virtual teams through video conferencing, fax and other electronic means. These cross-border business teams will be responsible for leveraging corporate capabilities throughout the world.

The proliferation of different channels for both consumer and business products, from club stores to distribution alliances to direct marketing, might pressure manufacturers to offer broad and varied product lines. In addition to these diverse ways of reaching customers, logistics management also includes the relationships with suppliers to get the right parts and products to your company as effectively and efficiently as possible. These factors can have a profound and strategic impact on the success of a product manager's offering.

> Just how strategic? Compaq Computer, the white-hot company that recently became the world's No. 1 producer of PCs, estimates it lost $500 million to $1 billion in sales [in 1994] because its laptops and desktops weren't available when and where customers were ready to buy them. Says chief financial officer Daryl White: "We've done most of what we need to do to be more competitive. We've changed the way we develop products, manufacture, market, and advertise. The one piece of the puzzle we haven't addressed is logistics. It's the next source of competitive advantage. The possibilities are just astounding."[7]

Product managers must realize the impact of the distribution channel (both in and out of the company) in affecting the success of the product line. The implication for the product manager is the need to solicit input from a wider spectrum of "customers" including suppliers, purchasing staff, and logistics and transportation personnel.

## Concluding Remarks

Product management is here to stay. The position is challenging, demanding, and rewarding. Product managers will be given more responsibilities as the challenges of going to market increase. Some companies will experiment with product management teams or a narrowing of job focus for product managers or a business unit approach, but the companies for whom the structure is most successful will hire, groom and enable product managers to create products with both internal integrity from a design perspective and external integrity from a customer perspective.

Regardless of the organizational changes product management goes through in the future, successful product managers will have a thorough understanding of the various segments within a market (including global segments), an understanding of the "core competencies" available to the company, and the ability to leverage these competencies to meet market needs. In other words, the product manager of the future will have the ability to attain customer satisfaction through being a cross-functional leader in the firm.

## References

1. Brian Dumaine, "The Trouble with Teams," *Fortune,* September 5, 1994, 88.

2. Ibid., 88-90.

3. Tracy Carlson, "Brand Burnout," *Brandweek,* January 17, 1994, 26.

4. Zachary Schiller, Wendy Zellner, Ron Stodghill, Mark Maremont, "Clout!" *Business Week,* December 21, 1992, 70.

5. Carlson, p. 27.

6. David Arnold, *The Handbook of Brand Management* (Addison-Wesley, 1992), p. 226.

7. Ronald Henkoff, "Delivering the Goods," *Fortune,* November 28, 1994, 64.

# Case Four

## The 3M ScotchCart® II Cartridge

The 3M ScotchCart®II cartridge was a broadcast cartridge tape for prerecorded radio messages introduced in 1986 by 3M's broadcasting and related products department. Product manager Bill Parfitt developed a marketing plan for it that highlighted the tactics most appropriate for increasing the cartridge's sales volume. According to Parfitt: "You must have a marketing plan to follow to be effective. With a plan, you are 90 percent proactive and 10 percent reactive. Without a plan, you are 90 percent reactive and 10 percent proactive. Even if a plan is not required, do one. It will save a tremendous amount of work."

The marketing tactics called for sales support products/activities, flexible pricing policies, trade shows, and print advertising.

### Sales Support

3M's toolbox of support items for the sales force was extensive. (See "Support Materials Supplied to Sales Force by 3M.") Some of these were provided routinely, while others were developed and made available on an as-needed basis. The product reference guide was an important piece of information for the sales force. It contained a brief product description, an opening sales statement, and opening and follow-up questions to help salespeople qualify needs. The next page of the reference guide contained common problems broadcasters might experience with tapes—and the resulting consequences—to enable the reps to customize the 3M product to the customer's needs. Although not all items are used with each product, many of these were provided for the ScotchCart®II cartridge.

As part of the marketing tactics, Parfitt made sure the sales force was informed of marketing activities before they were seen by the customer, and they always received a sample of giveaways in advance.

## Support Materials Supplied to Sales Force by 3M

- Comprehensive product/ application/market manuals
- History timelines
- Brochures
- Advertisement reprints
- Article reprints
- Technical bulletins
- Competitive comparisons
- Promotion outlines
- Product reference guide
- Newsletters
- Complete set of policy pages
- Complete dealer information
- Information on special accounts
- Complete pricing including special pricing
- List of key accounts or new prospects
- Buying pattern information
- Market research data
- Competitive brochures, ads, PR, etc.
- Glossary of industry terms
- Video training tapes
- Yearbooks
- Directories
- Flow charts
- Market application charts

## Flexible Pricing Policies

Radio stations, the target market for these 3M products, including the ScotchCart®II, were under pressure to conserve working capital while also needing to acquire sophisticated, technologically advanced equipment. 3M responded with several extended payment plans. The standard lease offered 36, 48 or 60-month pay-for-use plans on total purchases exceeding $5,000. The options available at the end of the lease included purchasing the equipment for the estimated market value, renewing the lease, or returning the equipment. The prime rate lease purchase plan provided financing for a 12- to 36-month term, with the title to the equipment transferring automatically upon completion of the final payment; the interest rate for the program was based on the current prime lending rate published each day in *The Wall Street Journal.*

In addition to the lease program, 3M used price actively in gaining customers both directly and through distribution. Special prices were developed for customer-special versions, partially based on the added value to the customers. Monetary incentives were also used to encourage dealers to switch their broadcasting customers from a competitive product to a 3M product. A 5% switcher/finder's fee was allocated for this purpose.

### Trade Shows

Trade shows were also used as a tactic for gaining awareness and preference for the product. Parfitt started by compiling a list of shows relevant to the potential market for the ScotchCart®II and then obtaining performance data on the shows.

Several decisions had to be made regarding the potential attendance at the trade shows. Should inquiry cards or brochures be provided? How many? Should giveaways, incentives or contests be part of the plan? What types? Should a pre-show mailer be sent to potential attendees? Who will be responsible for each activity?

Recognizing that trade shows are more than 3-dimensional ads, Parfitt put together a trade show plan. For an example of the type of planning tool that can be used, see "Trade Show Responsibilities." This information not only highlights the activities that need to be controlled for an effective trade show, but also lists the individuals responsible for making them happen.

**Trade Show Responsibilities**

| Description | Responsible | Projected completion date | Date completed |
|---|---|---|---|
| Setting objectives | | | |
| Gather show information | | | |
| Show selection | | | |
| Contract for space | | | |
| Exhibit design | | | |
| Exhibit construction | | | |
| Freight | | | |
| Drayage | | | |
| Set-up | | | |
| Electrical | | | |
| Plumbing | | | |
| Telephone | | | |
| Furniture rental | | | |
| Janitorial service | | | |
| Photography | | | |
| Guard service | | | |
| Florist service | | | |
| A/V equipment | | | |
| Presenters/models | | | |
| Inquiry cards | | | |
| Literature | | | |
| Equipment | | | |
| Badges | | | |
| Rooms | | | |
| Directory copy | | | |
| Suite | | | |
| Invitations | | | |
| Pre-show promotion | | | |
| Booth staffing | | | |
| Prizes | | | |
| Give-aways | | | |
| Budget projection | | | |
| Show evaluation form | | | |
| Inquiry follow-up | | | |
| Post-show follow-up | | | |
| Audit and pay related invoices | | | |
| Misc. | | | |

### Print Advertising

The advertising for the ScotchCart®II cartridge was designed to emphasize that the product lasted longer than the competition while delivering consistently high performance. In the ads the product was centrally-positioned with significant features pointed out through the use of arrows. *Business Marketing* evaluated the first ad of this series in its Copy Chasers column:

> 3M, always a strong contender in any advertising judging, caught our eye with an excellent invitation to "Discover the secrets to a longer life" for its broadcast cartridges (tape cartridges carrying prerecorded radio station messages, commercials and the like). The product cutaway and call-outs tell the entire product feature story, backing up the promise in the headline.[1]

Two other ads in the campaign continued the use of consistent layout and message. All carried the headline on top, the product cutaway in the center with call-out features on each side, two columns of copy at the bottom, with the 3M logo in the bottom right corner.

In order to get approval on the marketing communications expenditure required, Parfitt used supporting effectiveness ratios from an Advertising Research Foundation study. A formula built on this information was presented in *Business Marketing* for estimating return on promotional investment. The ROPI formula is:

Leads × Inserts × Buyers (45%) ×
Market share % × Average sales amount = Sales

The 45% figure in the formula is based on the results of two studies. The Inquiry Handling Service Inc., in analyzing 10,000 leads from 15 different business-to-business companies found that

21 percent bought some company's product within six months and 31 percent were still budgeted to buy within the year. A prior Advertising Research Foundation report (Report No. 25) cited similar ratios of buyers. The number of leads per insert is based on the uniqueness of the product, the effectiveness of the insert and similar variables; your best estimate of the figure can be obtained from past experience. The market share and average sales amount can be obtained from internal documents.

According to James Obermayer:

> The rules for the ROPI are simple: 22% or slightly more, of inquirers will buy within six months; around 45% of them will buy someone's product within one year. Furthermore, your company's share of those sales will usually be your market share in the industry.
>
> For example, suppose each insertion (magazine insertions or direct mail waves) produces 30 leads and the media plan calls for 12 insertions. We expect 45% of those leads to buy within a year. Knowing or estimating market share at 36%, and knowing the average sale produces $950 revenue, we forecast total sales of $55,404 from the leads generated by the ads. From that point, it's very easy to predict cost per raw lead and a cost per closed lead.[2]
>
> Several techniques were built into the program to help track the campaign. Bingo cards (reply cards inserted into a publication for readers to request literature from companies whose products and services are advertised) were used where appropriate. In other cases, steps were taken to ensure inquiries were routed to the product manager.

# DISCOVER THE SECRETS TO A LONGER LIFE.

*Naturally lubricated concave guides gently position tape to allow cartridge machine to perform critical guidance.*

*High-output, low-noise, 100% laser-inspected tape delivers impressive frequency response and higher recording levels for better signal-to-noise performance.*

*Non-rotating hub reduces wow and flutter, eliminates annoying rotating hub rattle and minimizes stop cue overshoot.*

*Adjustable cam to control tape loop for maximum life.*

*Cover constructed of polycarbonate materials for long-lasting, break-resistant use.*

*No pressure pads to cause troublesome tape steering and wear or induce modulation noise.*

*Patented dynamic tension control system ensures proper tape-to-head contact, provides constant tape tension and controls tape looping.*

*Tape exits from the hub's center instead of twisting and curling over the pack, reducing edge stress and debris to prolong life.*

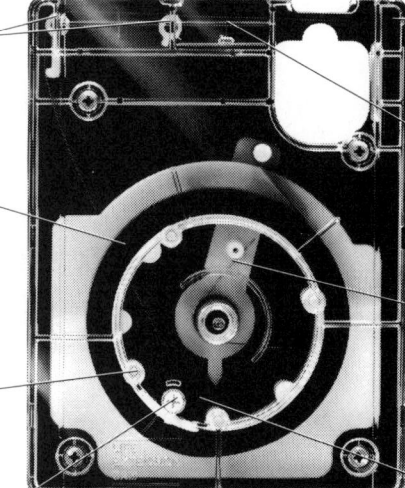

*The ScotchCart® II Cartridge*

A broadcast cartridge that lasts longer isn't worth much unless it delivers consistently high performance throughout its useful life. That's why the revolutionary design of the ScotchCart® II cartridge is noticeably superior to other carts.'

It also sounds better because of 3M's extensive audio tape experience—over 40 years of successful innovation.

So if you measure a cart's value by how much

trouble-free operation it provides in the long run, talk to your professional audio dealer or local 3M sales office about the advantages of the ScotchCart® II cartridge.

Or, if you'd like a free sample, call International Tapetronics, 3M Broadcasting and Related Products Department at 800-447-0414. (In Alaska or Illinois, call collect 309-828-1381.)

It's no mystery why it performs better. Longer.

# HOW REDUCING STRESS IMPROVES JOB PERFORMANCE.

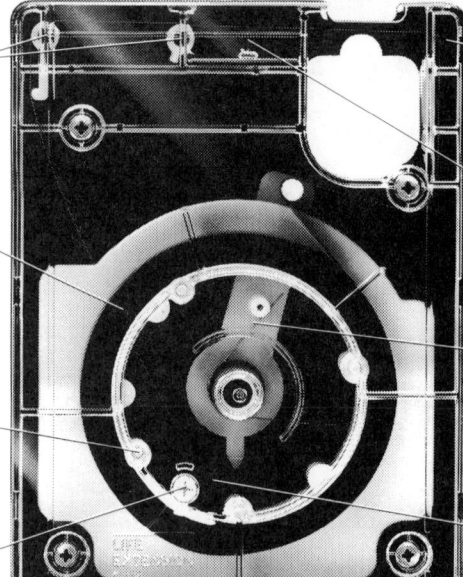

Naturally lubricated concave guides gently position tape to allow cartridge machine to perform critical guidance.

High-output, low-noise, 100% laser-inspected tape delivers impressive frequency response and higher recording levels for better signal-to-noise performance.

Non-rotating hub reduces wow and flutter, eliminates annoying rotating hub rattle and minimizes stop cue overshoot.

Adjustable cam to control tape loop for maximum life.

Cover constructed of polycarbonate materials for long-lasting, break-resistant use.

No pressure pads to cause troublesome tape steering and wear or induce modulation noise.

Patented dynamic tension control system ensures proper tape-to-head contact, provides constant tape tension and controls tape looping.

Tape exits from the hub's center instead of twisting and curling over the pack, reducing edge stress and debris to prolong life.

*The ScotchCart* II Cartridge*

The reason most broadcast cartridges quickly become unreliable and self-destruct isn't because they're overused. Poor designs that create too much friction and tape stress can cause more headaches than anything. But as you can see, the revolutionary design of ScotchCart* II cartridges makes them noticeably superior to other carts.

They also sound better because of 3M's extensive audio tape experience—over 40 years of successful innovation and product development.

So if you measure a cart's value by how much trouble-free performance it provides in the long run, talk to your professional audio dealer or local 3M sales office about the advantages of using ScotchCart* II cartridges. Or for a free sample, call International Tapetronics, 3M Broadcasting and Related Products Department at 800-447-0414. (In Alaska or Illinois, call collect 309-828-1381.)

The ScotchCart* II cartridge from 3M. The one you can depend on to keep things running smoothly.

**3M**

# WHY YOU SHOULD PAY MORE FOR LESS.

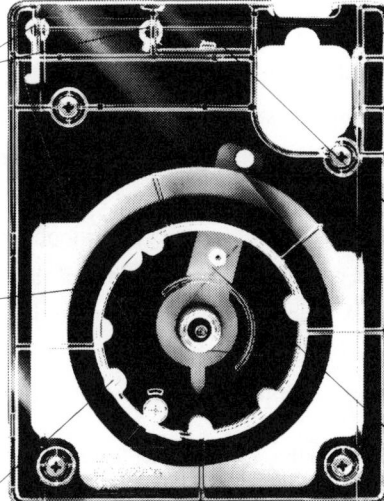

*Less phase jitter caused by poorly tracking tape, because the naturally lubricated concave guides gently position the tape and allow the cartridge machine to perform critical guidance.*

*Less chance of the cartridge cracking or breaking, because the tough polycarbonate cover withstands repeated use and abuse.*

*Less tape noise and signal loss with our 100% laser-inspected, high output, low noise tape which delivers better frequency response and keeps signal-to-noise ratio high, harmonic distortion low.*

*Less head wear, tape steering and modulation noise, because there aren't any pressure pads to add friction.*

*Less wow and flutter or stop cue overshoot, because there's no rotating hub to wear out, warp or rattle.*

*The ScotchCart II Cartridge*

*Less chance of tape destruction, because our patented dynamic tension control system ensures proper tape-to-head contact, and provides constant tension to control looping and prevent twisting.*

With broadcast cartridges, like everything else, you get what you pay for. With ScotchCart'II cartridges, you get a revolutionary design that delivers trouble-free operation, superb sound quality and a life expectancy that's second to none.

You also get the benefit of 3M's extensive audio tape experience—over 40 years of successful innovation and product development.

So if you measure a cart's value by how much uncompromising performance it provides in the long run, talk to your professional audio dealer or local 3M sales office about the advantages of the ScotchCart'II cartridge. Or for a free sample, call International Tapetronics, 3M Broadcasting and Related Products Department at 800-447-0414. (In Alaska or Illinois, call collect 309-828-1381.)

Because a cheaper cartridge may be more trouble than you can afford.

## Conclusion

The marketing tactics for the ScotchCart®II as well as other 3M products were based on an integrated approach to planning. Objectives
were established to guide the implementation of the plan. All possible
promotional vehicles were considered as viable elements of the marketing communications. Pricing was built into the plan rather than
simply being an after-the-plan reaction. And finally, sales promotion,
in the form of free sampling, was incorporated to help the market gain
rapid experience with the product.

As for other product managers, the message is clear. The first step
is to identify the problems and opportunities for a given product that
should trigger planning items for the next fiscal year. These problems
and opportunities must then be converted into objectives for the marketing plan. Based on the objectives, a target market must be selected
for the product and a positioning strategy developed to differentiate
the product from the competition in the minds of that target market.
Finally, specific tactics (pricing, marketing communications, logistics,
product support) need to be acted on to solidify the positioning in the
customers' minds and accomplish the fiscal year objectives.

Source: Adapted from a workshop conducted by Bill Parfitt, June 7, 1991; and
3M promotional materials.

## References

1. "Copy Chasers" column, *Business Marketing,* March 1989, 90-92.

2. James W. Obermayer, "Marrying Communications to Sales
   Dollars," *Business Marketing,* July 1988, 71.

# GLOSSARY

**Action program.** The part of the marketing plan describing the actual steps by which the marketing strategy is implemented to reach the established objectives.

**Alpha test.** A method of testing a new product prototype within the developing company to eliminate potential defects before commercial launch. For example, a manufacturer of accounting software might test a new product within its own accounting department.

**Benchmarking.** Comparing a product, a product feature, or a process against best-in-class to improve the level of quality.

**Beta test.** A method of testing a new product prototype under actual customer use situations to eliminate potential defects before commercial launch.

**Brand equity.** The goodwill or positive identity of a brand.

**Brand extension.** A slight variation of a product, carrying the brand name of the core product.

**Brand manager.** The product manager title frequently used in consumer packaged goods.

**Category killers.** Large-scale companies that have changed the way business is done in their industries by operating more cost effectively. For example, Wal-Mart in retailing, Home Depot in do-it-yourself home improvement, and W. W. Grainger in industrial distribution.

**Causal forecasts.** Forecasts developed by studying the cause-and-effect relationships between variables. For example, housing starts might have a causal effect on the demand for private mortgage insurance.

**Competitive intelligence.** The process of gathering, analyzing, and disseminating information on the competitive environment obtained through sales force input, on-line database searching, published sources, personal interviews, etc.

**Concept screening.** The evaluation of new product ideas to determine whether they merit further analysis and development.

**Concept testing.** The activity of taking new product ideas to customers for their input before further development.

**Continuity.** Advertising on a continuous basis to the target market.

**Contribution margin.** The amount of revenue left after incremental costs have been subtracted.

**Contribution to overhead (CTO).** The line on an income statement that indicates the amount of revenue left to cover overhead and profit after all direct and controllable costs have been subtracted.

**Core competencies.** The central skills and knowledge of a company that provide its strengths against competition.

**Customer visit program.** A method of qualitative marketing research whereby product managers visit customers as part of a team with the sole purpose of collecting market information (such as ideas for new products).

**Delphi technique.** A method of reconciling subjective forecasts by using a sequential series of estimates derived from a panel of experts. Often used in forecasting technological change.

**Distribution channel.** The set of all the firms and individuals that take title, or assist in transferring title, to a particular product or service as it moves from the producer to the customer.

**Early indicator chart.** A chart of "red flags" that might indicate that a new product launch is not moving at the pace required in the launch materials.

**Fixed costs.** Costs that don't vary with production or sales level. Rent, heat and executive salaries are examples of fixed costs.

**Flanker brands.** Products created to reach a new market segment without altering the positioning of the main brand. For example, a new product or brand might be created for a low-priced segment of the market rather than reducing the price of the core product.

**FMCG.** Fast-moving consumer goods.

**Focus group.** A semi-structured, free-flowing interview with a small group of customers, usually for the purpose of obtaining qualitative research.

**Frame of reference.** The set of products a customer considers when making a purchase decision in a given product category.

**Frequency.** The average number of times a customer sees an advertising message within a given time period.

**Gross margin.** Sales revenue less cost of goods sold.

**Incremental costs.** Costs that change with a decision to produce an additional quantity of product. These would include direct costs plus any semi-fixed costs (such as adding an additional shift) resulting from an increase in quantity produced.

**Launch.** The introduction of new product to the market.

**Launch control plan.** The identification of activities to be performed as part of new product commercialization, as well as the recognition of "red flags" to look for during the process.

**Market segmentation.** The process of breaking a group of potential customers into smaller, more homogenous subsets.

**Matrix organization.** An organizational structure in which individuals have both direct line (i.e., functional) reporting relationships as well as responsibilities to work horizontally with other groups in the company.

**Milestone activities chart.** A list of the desired dates of completion for various "milestone" activities of a new product launch such as purchasing equipment, finalizing package design, obtaining legal clearance, etc.

**New product proposal.** A summary of a business plan for a new product concept.

**Parity.** Being perceived the same as all competitors, such as with commodity products.

**Perceptual map.** A visual depiction of how customers position a product versus its competitors along identified factors.

**Positioning statement.** A statement of how a product offering is to be perceived in the minds of customers relative to the competition.

**Price sensitivity.** The degree to which a target market is motivated by price in making purchase decisions.

**Product fact book.** A compilation of all information a company has on a product, its customers, and the product's competitors.

**Product management team.** A cross-functional group used by some companies to make product management decisions in lieu of or in conjunction with product managers.

**Prototype.** A mock-up or preliminary version of a new product used for research purposes.

**Pulsing.** Grouping marketing communications within a given period of time to provide more intensity or impact than could be obtained from spreading those same communications evenly throughout the year.

**Reach.** The number or percent of the target market being exposed to an advertising message within a given time period.

**Regression.** A statistical method of relating a causal variable, such as an economic indicator, to sales. Future sales are then forecast by inserting the estimated causal variable into the equation.

**Return on promotional investment (ROPI).** A calculation of revenue generated directly from marketing communications, expressed as a percentage of the investment in those communications.

**Roll-out.** The process of introducing a new product to the market by selectively prioritizing the markets and the order in which they receive the new product.

**Segment management.** The process of organizing internal decisions and job roles by market segment rather than by product or function.

**Share.** The portion of the overall sales in a market accounted for by a particular product, brand, or service. Also referred to as market share or share-of-market (SOM).

**Standard Industrial Classification (SIC).** Numeric government codes assigned to companies to designate the industry they are in.

**Target market.** A market or portion of a market that a firm attempts to serve by actively allocating resources to it. Sometimes referred to as served market.

**Test marketing.** Taking a new product to a limited number of cities, companies, or geographic regions to test the effectiveness of a marketing strategy before the product is launched.

**Unique selling proposition (USP).** A term used to describe the primary competitive differentiation of a product or service to be addressed in marketing communications.

**Variable costs.** Those costs that vary directly with the level of production. They tend to be constant per unit produced.

# COMPANY INDEX

# Subject Index

# TITLES OF INTEREST IN MARKETING, DIRECT MARKETING, AND SALES PROMOTION

For further information or a current catalog, write:
NTC Business Books
a division of *NTC Publishing Group*
4255 West Touhy Avenue
Lincolnwood, Illinois 60646–1975 U.S.A.